Their wo

Your words

By Debbie Waller

their world your words

 ISBN-13: 978-0-9954599-5-3

Published by Ann Jaloba Publishing, 26 Tapton Mount Close, Sheffield S10 5DJ

DEDICATION

For my family, without whose emotional - and practical - support I would have never considered writing a book: my Mum, my beautiful girls Rachel and Katharine and, of course, David, my rock as always.

their world your words

CONTENTS

Foreword *ii*
About the author *v*
Introduction *vii*

1. Getting into your client's world 13

2. Exploring your client's world 37

3. Changing your client's world 57

4. Working with words 75

5. Words, stories and metaphors 111

6. When worlds collide 127

Appendix One: SMART Goals *145*
Appendix Two: Client Intake Details *147*
Appendix Three: Transference & Counter-transference *154*
Appendix Four: Stress Account *159*
Other resources *160*
References *163*
Index *167*

Foreword

Debbie Waller trains hypnotherapists. This book grew out of the inevitable debates that such training raises around the use of hypnosis scripts. As a trainer she produced guidance notes in response to questions asked by her students. The end result is the book that you are now reading.

Scripts are an important part of the hypnotherapist's tool-bag, but used indiscriminately and as written, by someone who has never and will never meet your clients, they can cause more harm than good. They can also be surprisingly ineffective. There's little worse for the hypnotherapist, using as they do, some of the world's most powerful techniques to bring about change, than being ineffective.

Scripts as supplied can contain phrases that you would never use in normal conversation. This can result in you ending up sounding like a contrived version of yourself. Clients, in their suggestible state, would pick this up. As the most important parts of communication are non-verbal you can end up achieving the opposite of what you set out to. As an experienced hypnotherapist myself, first training in 1987, I've seen too many therapists rely on scripts as written. They end up being less effective than they should otherwise have been, or worse, doing such an unimpressive job that they put the client off hypnotherapy for ever.

A basic principle of hypnotherapy is to 'use what the client gives you'. A client passively subjected to scripts does not contribute much to the therapeutic process. Debbie Waller addresses this by emphasising the importance of personalising a script to suit the client. This is useful as many therapists provide their clients with recordings for them to use between sessions in order to boost the suggestions given. Repetition in suggestion therapy is important as it takes a while for suggestions to become sublimated to the point where the client no longer has to invest conscious thought into maintaining a new behaviour, feeling or habit. As the author has herself stated on numerous training days, you can't adapt the scripts to an individual if you haven't asked the right questions.

When all is said and done though a script remains a tool. No apology for throwing in the cliché that any craftsman is only as good as their tools! There is no inherent link between having a lot of scripts making you any more effective a hypnotherapist than a bagful of wrenches automatically making you a better plumber. That's achieved by training and experience. Part of that training and experience should be challenging scripts. A good hypnotherapist adapts a script to suit a client, a great hypnotherapist learns everything that there is to know about scripts and then moves beyond them.

In producing this book, Debbie has given you the tools to become a great hypnotherapist.

Michael O'Sullivan

About Michael

Mike is a former director and founder of The Emergency Services Trauma Specialists, a charity providing education, training and services to the emergency services and their families following involvement in critical incidents. The charity came to a natural conclusion after many other organisations began offering those same services and a specialist charity was no longer deemed necessary. A resounding success story.

Mike is a Fellow of the National Council of Psychotherapists (NCP) and of the National Council for Hypnotherapy (NCH). He was co-author of *The Hypnotherapy Resources & Careers Guide*, a breakthrough publication when it first appeared helping potential hypnotherapists find their way into the profession.

Today Mike concentrates his efforts on providing quality distance learning courses.

About the Author

I became a hypnotherapist pretty much by accident, shortly after completing my degree as a 'mature student' and finding myself in a position of having lots of education, but no saleable skills. I had left school without any idea of what I wanted to do with my life and ended up in a fairly routine office job. Having taken time off to look after the kids and get the degree, I wanted to do something more meaningful.

I was looking for training that would enable me to employ myself, and my husband suggested attending the open day of a local hypnotherapy school. I went with no prior knowledge or experience, got hooked and the rest, as they say, is history.

Since then hypnotherapy has been my only career, though I'm still learning more every day and have added related skills such as stress management, a form of EMDR known as the BLAST technique, and coaching.

I've worked part time and full time, as my family commitments allowed, and loved every minute. My clients are the most wonderful people, facing their situations with such courage and commitment that I am overcome with admiration. Who wouldn't want a job like that?

I'm currently a therapist, hypnotherapy trainer and supervisor. That is a lot of different roles but I think it's essential to be working regularly with clients if you are training and supervising therapists. That is the only way to share their experiences out there in the 'real world'.

I'm also a blogger, contributor to *The Hypnotherapy Handbook* and contributor/editor of *Hypnotherapy Training and Practitioner*, an online magazine.

I am registered at Advanced level with the General Hypnotherapy Register, at Senior level with the British Institute of Hypnotherapy and NLP, as a Senior Member with the ACCPH and as an Accredited Stress Coach with the Stress Coaching Association. All are the highest levels of membership available.

I established Yorkshire Hypnotherapy Training in 2011, after several years of teaching for other hypnotherapy training providers. The school has developed an excellent reputation, and I am very proud of its many graduates now in practice.

This book is for them, and for everyone out there who is still training or recently graduated. And I hope that it can be useful to experienced hypnotherapists who feel they need a new approach.

Introduction

In recent years there seems to have been an explosion of books and websites offering scripts for the practising hypnotherapist, so there is obviously a demand. But on social media and in other places where members of the profession gather, scripts are a topic of heated debate. There are those who would never enter a client session without a script, and those who believe they inhibit the creativity which is at the heart of any good hypnotherapy session.

As with so many things, there is a middle ground. Immersing yourself in hypnotic language is a much easier way to learn it than committing a list of rules to memory. Not only that, we are not all natural 'off-the-cuff' story-tellers, and although it's a skill that can be acquired, it takes time to be confident. Those still learning or new to the amazing world of hypnotherapy often worry about 'going blank' in the middle of a session. Using a script to give you ideas, but blending it with your own material based upon the client's unique situation seems to be a good way to go.

This is the general principle I've always given my students; it wasn't until last year that one of them said to me, 'It's all very well saying, "Adapt the scripts to the person you're working with", but how? What should I put in there from all the information they've given me? Where should I put it?'

I realised at once that she had a point and went looking for ideas that might offer some sort of structure or guidance. I couldn't find any, and it was the beginning of this book.

My original thought was what a friend called 'scripts with holes', alongside notes about what to put in them. That idea had its merits, and it may yet happen, but I soon realised when I started writing that I couldn't start there. I had to take a step back and talk about how to collect the right information from your client before I could talk about what to do with it. And so *Their Worlds, Your Words* was born.

What I hope you now have in your hand is a kind of pocket guide to creating effective scripts and sessions, something which will give you structure without stifling your individual style and flair, and which will give you ideas and approaches so you can tap into the many wonderful scripts that are around, and still make every session personal and relevant to your clients.

It just remains for me to say a few thank yous.

To Ann Jaloba for her wise words and advice as I worked my way through this project. To Verena, Lynne, Kim, Kathleen and others who gave me feedback and ideas as it grew.

And most of all to my students, who obviously teach me as much as I teach them.

Debbie

Chapter One

Getting into your client’s world

The first step to creating effective session content is building the right relationship with your client. Rapport is the word often used to describe this relationship, which is made up of elements like compatibility, trust and emotional affinity.

The first step to creating effective session content is building the right relationship with your client. Rapport is the word often used to describe this relationship, which is made up of elements like compatibility, trust and emotional affinity.

We sometimes say we are ‘in rapport with' friends, family and others that we feel close to or confide in, but this usually comes about over time through two-way communication. This will include shared confidences, experiences, feelings and values. In therapy, rapport has to come from a different place because you don't have the same kind of interaction with clients.

Your clients' experiences and feelings, even values, may be completely different from yours and yet they need to feel that they can safely share personal information with you, and talk about difficult experiences or emotions without you being shocked or judgemental.

They may not have revealed some of these things to anyone else before, or even admitted them to themselves. This requires you to build a deep level of trust - what we call rapport - quickly and effectively.

At the same time, you need to maintain enough professional distance to be able to help your clients without being overwhelmed by the cumulative effect of listening to so many emotional stories. This means not sharing much about yourself or getting as closely involved as you might with a friend.

It's a delicate balancing act, usually described in terms of empathy and sympathy. Sympathy can be described as feeling 'for' the client and empathy as feeling 'with' them.

As an example, imagine a client tells you they feel 'weak-willed and guilty' because their many past attempts to quit smoking have failed. Sympathy means understanding that struggling to quit is making them feel bad, perhaps even remembering how you felt when you failed at something. You feel sorry for them, and/or want them to feel better.

Knowing people are sympathetic can sometimes bring comfort, but for a therapist it's not enough to offer. For one thing, you cannot be expected to have experienced every situation or feeling you will work with over your career. More importantly, how you might feel in their situation is not necessarily how they feel, even if they use the same or similar words to describe it. And if their feeling is different, their best solution is likely to be different as well.

Empathy means understanding things as if you were the other person, rather than as if you were in their situation instead of them. Arguably you can never know exactly what another person is feeling, but if you understand as closely as possible what your client is experiencing when they 'feel weak-willed and guilty', you can help them to find the right solutions for them.

Hopefully, you can begin to see that as therapists we are aiming to build rapport via empathy rather than sympathy. It helps us to understand our clients' points of view so we can help them more effectively to achieve the changes they want in the right way for them. This means not only finding ways to 'get into the client's world', but demonstrating that we have done this so that they can then trust the help we can offer. And the secret to doing this is good communication.

NLP (Neuro-Linguistic Programming) tells us that we can't *not* communicate. Even if you were to sit quietly and still in a corner, without making eye contact, moving around or speaking, other people would put an interpretation on what was going on: maybe they'd think you were being rude, sulking, wanting to be alone, or upset. Everything we choose to do or not to do sends a message, and communication is not just words.

We're going to look at some areas of communication which will help you to build your relationship with your client, understand how they experience the world, and gather the right information to provide effective session content which will help them regain control of their lives.

Non-verbal communication

Non-verbal communication, or NVC, is the term which has

largely taken over from 'body language'. Body language is certainly a part of NVC, but there is much more to it than that. It includes any communication which is not words. Some non-verbal communications, like waving, can be used consciously, but it is often an unconscious process. A person who is impaired in their ability to use or recognise NVC (for example, because of a condition such as autism) is often thought to have a reduced ability to be understood or to communicate with others. As a quick aside, it can also be a factor in some social and public speaking phobias since we do not receive NVC feedback from a group in the same way that we receive it from individuals.

According to Edward Wertheim[1] non-verbal communication can

- repeat the message the person is sending verbally e.g. smiling when you say how much you like something
- contradict a message the person is sending verbally e.g. saying 'it's the truth' but using a defensive tone and not making eye contact
- replace a verbal message e.g. waving, nodding or smiling as a greeting
- add to or complement a verbal message e.g. giving someone a hug as you say you love them
- emphasise a verbal message e.g. banging on the table to emphasise a point

He also suggests that NVC can be divided into four basic groups:

- visual
- tactile
- vocal
- use of time, space and images

Let's have a look at each of these in turn and see how

they can help you build your relationship with your client. Many of them, nodding, smiling, posture and so on, are also often used to indicate you are paying attention to your client without interrupting the flow of their thoughts or conversation, but we'll look at those aspects in more detail when we discuss listening skills.

Visual NVCs are the kind that can be seen, of course, and may also be called body language. They include waving, smiling, flinching, posture, expression, gestures, eye contact and gaze direction. Reading, or at least being aware of, your client's body language is essential to good communication, but being in control of your own NVCs can be even more important. If a client is telling you about an experience that was terrifying or upsetting, or confessing to an action they feel ashamed of, a calm response and facial expression will reassure them that they are right to confide in you because they are not being judged.

Tactile NVCs are those that use touch and physical contact, so they include handshakes, hugs, and touching your client's hand to set an anchor, or to indicate a yes/no finger for use as an Ideo-Motor Signal. Some people are naturally more tactile than others and this is a matter for personal preference, but if you want to build and keep rapport with your clients you will take many of your cues from them. Hugging a person who prefers to be 'hands off' can be misconstrued at worst, or make them feel uncomfortable at best. Dodging or refusing a 'thank you' hug at the end of therapy can make a more tactile person feel slighted or rejected.

Vocal NVCs are all aspects of spoken communication, except the words themselves. This is sometimes referred to as 'paralanguage' and includes tone, pitch, quality of voice, rate of speaking, and absence of speaking or silences. This is a huge part of understanding language, for example how many different uses can you think of for the words 'yes' and 'no' which depend entirely on the tone of voice? It's why texts and emails can be misunderstood at times, although they do seem to have developed a kind of paralanguage of their own based in emoticons and exaggerated punctuation. If your friend does something silly, sending 'idiot ☺' or 'idiot(!!!)' is not the same as sending 'idiot'.

Silences in particular can be very powerful in therapy. Rushing in to fill the silence with your next question or comment can jolt the client out of a contemplative state of mind which could have led to powerful insights and progress. You can use a pause in the conversation to give a client time to decide what to say next, experience an emotion, get their heads around an idea or to just switch off the jangle of thoughts in their minds. And of course, especially when in trance, silences allow the client to process what they are experiencing.

Use of time, space and images covers a wide variety of areas that you might not even think of as NVC. For example, have you ever turned up for an appointment on time, only to be kept waiting for ages, then seen with no explanations or apologies for the delay? What about if a client books an appointment with you and fails to show? How does that make you feel? Frustrated? Angry? Disrespected? How do you think your client feels if you book an appointment with them and then keep them hanging around?

Hopefully your answers to these questions will show you that the way in which we use time: our own and other people's, can send a message, especially about how we value them and ourselves. And if it's sending a message without words, then it is a type of non-verbal communication.

Our use of space in our therapy room communicates in a similar way: you would never push your client's chair into a corner with your own directly in front of them, blocking their view of the room. Sitting behind a desk might make you seem formal and professional, or distant and inaccessible. A couple of chairs at around a 45 degree angle can be more friendly and comfortable, allowing your client to make eye contact when they want to, or to break that contact simply by shifting their gaze if they want a moment to process something that's been said.

Personal space, which refers to how close you like people to stand when you are talking, is also part of spatial NVC. This can be cultural, but may also help you to judge the levels of

Try this out: the lift

Watch how people's NVC changes when they are forced to stand closer together than usual, for example in a lift.

Try this out: stand there

Hold a conversation with someone standing slightly further away than you normally would; notice how it makes you feel and how the other person reacts. Then hold a conversation standing closer than normal, and observe what changes for both of you. (To avoid making anyone else feel awkward, it's a good idea to tell the other person you're experimenting with personal space before doing this.)

anxiety your client is experiencing. Years ago, I had a client whose first move was always to rearrange the chairs in my office to what was, for him, a comfortable distance. As his anxiety decreased, so did his personal space. Wertheim (ibid. page 3) says of Americans that the 'personal zone' from about 2-4 feet usually is reserved for family and friends. The 'social zone' (4- 12 feet) is where most business transactions take place. The 'public zone' (over 12 feet) is used for lectures.

The use of images as NVC refers to a kind of extension of the visual variety, and includes elements like personal presentation and environment. Whether you choose to dress for your clients in a formal suit, a white coat, jeans and a tee shirt, full Goth regalia or a long, flowing 'Harry Potter' type cloak complete with mysterious sigils, sparkly runes and a pointy hat, you are sending an image-based non-verbal message. The same can be said for the way you decorate your therapy room and the colours and images you choose for your website. There's nothing wrong with any of these approaches of course, and, whatever you decide on, you'll still get clients because that message will be attractive to someone (though the more extreme approaches could be somewhat limited in their appeal). But getting it right for the client base you're aiming to attract encourages your clients to feel at ease and open up to you.

The problem with non-verbal communication is that, although there are said to be seven universal human expressions (happiness, sadness, boredom, fear, anger, surprise and disgust), most are cultural or vary depending on the social groups we ally ourselves with. 'Thumbs up', for example, is a positive signal in the UK and America, but might be taken as a sexual insult elsewhere and is likely to be taken as an insult in West Africa or Afghanistan. Nodding the head up and down for yes and shaking it from side to side for no is common in the UK, but reversed in Bulgaria and Albania. How much eye contact is desirable is also very variable. It's something to bear in mind if you work with clients from a different cultural background from your own.

Professor Albert Mehrabian suggested that the way we interpret the meaning of communication breaks down like this:

- 7 % verbal: the actual words
- 38 % vocal (paralanguage): the way the words are spoken
- 55 % body language and movements: especially facial expressions/eyes[2]

Try this out: two truths and a lie

Ask someone to tell you three short stories or make three statements about themselves. Two should be true, and one should be completely false. (But not too unlikely. If someone says 'I have blue eyes, my last holiday was to Spain and I walked on the moon before Neil Armstrong' it's fairly obvious which is the lie!) Give them some time to decide what to say, without you watching. Then try to identify which is the lie by watching their NVCs. Is it easier to spot the false stories or the true statements?

Try this out: mime

Try this out: try to tell a story using only NVCs. You'll need to brush up on your mime skills for this one. Or try to tell a story without using any NVCs at all.

Mehrabian's figures are sometimes quoted as if the percentages remain consistent across all communications, but of course this is not the case. It's nonsensical to suggest that if you are getting spoken directions to the nearest car park you only give 7% of your attention to the words. If you are communicating by phone, text, or email some elements are not available to you, although as I said earlier, the use of punctuation, emoticons, etc. has arguably become a way of replacing NVC in those mediums.

Mehrabian was actually looking at communications in which people were expressing feelings and attitudes, and concluded that if different elements of the communication were incongruent (that is, they didn't match) the figures above applied. In other words if someone says one thing in words, and another with their NVCs, you will tend to trust the non-verbal cues considerably more than the verbal ones. This is probably because of the unconscious element; it's much harder to conceal or fake non-verbal communication than it is to say nothing or tell a fib. It also makes his findings very useful for therapists, since clients are often talking about feelings and attitudes. If a client says they are 'fine' for example, close observation of their NVCs may confirm this, or let you know that it may not actually be the case.

Listening skills

It's often said there's a big difference between hearing and listening. We all hear things said by other people every day, but we don't always listen to everything they are telling us. I hope our brief exploration of non-verbal communication has shown you that to really get into your client's world, you not only have to be aware of what they say, but the way in which they say it. The right kind of listening can be another way of doing this.

Scenario one: you are driving home in heavy traffic. Your kids are in the car and telling you all about their day. At any other time you'd be really interested but at the moment you are trying to pull out across a lane of oncoming traffic at a busy junction. You might make acknowledging noises like 'oh, yes' or 'uh huh' from time to time but your attention is on other things, and you're unlikely to retain a lot of what's being said. We could call this 'only-just listening', because although you are making some effort, not much of it's going in.

Scenario two: you are at a party chatting to someone you like. It's quite noisy and there are a lot of other people around. From time to time your attention is diverted as you wave a greeting to a new arrival across the room or hear your name mentioned in another conversation, but you feel you are focused on the person you're talking to. This is the kind of 'everyday listening' that most of us do most of the time.

Scenario three: you are listening to someone giving instructions about a job they want you to do. You make an effort to focus your attention on the other person and cut out any environmental distractions. At the same time, part of your mind is observing the conversation from the outside and making notes, perhaps about how you might carry out the instructions and any questions you want to ask later. This is 'attentive' or 'active' listening.

Scenario four: a friend is telling you about an adventure they had on holiday. The story is totally gripping and you find yourself effortlessly and completely caught up in it, feeling scared, anxious, or happy at all the right moments. You might feel you are unaware of time passing or of much that is going on around you. This is 'focused' listening, and you could argue that it's close to what we want of our clients when they're in trance.

Try this out: switch off

Ask someone to speak to you about their favourite TV programme or hobby and deliberately switch your own NVC between the levels. (It can be wise to warn them you are practicing your listening skills, but don't tell them exactly what you're going to do.) If they don't feel you are paying the right level of attention, many people either find it difficult to continue, or their own NVC changes. If they don't think you are listening enough they may come closer, speaking louder or more insistently to try to get your attention. If they feel you are too engrossed for the subject matter, they may feel uncomfortable and reduce the intensity.

Now, take a moment and think. If you were watching these four conversations without being able to hear them, how would you know what level of listening was gong on? I hope you answered non-verbal communication. Signals like eye contact, posture, proximity, facial expression, gaze direction and so on would make it quite easy to tell how much attention the listener was giving the speaker.

We've already said that when you listen to your clients you need to take in every level of meaning that you can from their communication. This helps you understand them more clearly, empathise with them more effectively and build a good level of rapport. It's also going to help you to build a personalised, effective hypnotic session for them.

This means you need to be at least using active listening. You may not reach the focused variety often, because at the same time as taking in what the client says you are also making mental or written notes, applying what you know to that information, thinking how you can use the information later in the session and what you need to pick up on or know more about, so part of your attention is on your own processing. Be careful not to let this take over, though, and slip into the less attentive levels of listening. If you are busy thinking 'I have the perfect script for that' and wondering where you filed it, you may miss an important piece of information.

Understanding your client's communications

NLP tells us that communication means both what is said and what is understood. This essentially means that if you or the client says something that has two potential meanings you have to come to an agreement on which is appropriate before you can really understand one another. The point of active listening is to make sure that both sides of the communication understand the same thing.

Let's imagine a client tells you the following: 'I've stopped smoking so many times before, it starts off really well but it never lasts. My partner stopped the first time he tried but I can't. I usually go about a week and then something bad happens. I feel stressed out and fed up and I just give in and go back to it. I'm ashamed of myself for losing control and having no willpower but I still do it.'

For conversational purposes this seems pretty clear and you could certainly offer your sympathy. But if you are going to use this information to help the client quit smoking you need empathy, not sympathy, which means making sure you've got more than just the gist of the message.

There are a number of prompts and feedback techniques you can use as part of your active listening to make sure that you understand how this situation feels to your client and begin to take things forward.

- **Paraphrasing** means putting what the client has told you into your own words and feeding them back. So you might say: 'You've stopped smoking successfully in the past but you find it hard to be a non-smoker in the longer term, especially when you are under pressure.' This lets the client know you were listening and taking in what she said, and if there are any discrepancies in what she meant and what you understood she can let you know.
- **Restating**, which is like paraphrasing but uses the client's own words instead of yours. This client has used several words and phrases which could mean different things to different people, such as 'stressed out', 'something bad' or 'no control'. If you don't want to risk misinterpreting them but don't want to interrupt the flow of her thoughts by asking about them directly, restating is the way to go. 'You have no control over your smoking if something bad happens or you are stressed out.' By using the client's own words you are avoiding an incorrect interpretation until you have more information.
- **Feeling reflections** are also similar to paraphrasing but instead of feeding back factual information, you feed back the emotions you think the client is communicating. 'It seems that when your attempt to stop smoking failed you felt guilty for not being stronger.' You may feel that this client has no real reason to feel guilty, but that isn't the issue. Remember that for empathy you need to understand how she feels without bringing your own judgements or ideas into the situation. Feeling reflections not only check your perceptions of the situation, they validate the client's feelings because you are accepting their reality.
- **Mirroring**, sometimes called synchronicity, is based on observations that when we are interacting positively with

others we often copy (mirror) their NVCs. Next time you get the chance, at a meeting or maybe when 'people watching' at a party, notice how if one person in a group puts their hand to their face, yawns or adjusts their posture in a particular way the others will often follow suit. You can use this to make your client feel comfortable and at home. If they are very tense you can pick up on some element of their language or behaviour and mirror it with your own, then gradually change your own to a more relaxed version, hoping they will follow your lead. This is called pacing and leading, and can be verbal, (for example, using the words they use to describe their situation, then gradually changing them to more positive ones), or non-verbal, (for example, based on their posture). So if your client sits bolt upright with their arms folded tight, you might sit up straighter than usual, maybe cross your wrists loosely in your lap, then after a while begin to relax your own posture and arms. If you have started to build rapport they will follow your lead and begin to relax. If not, mirror for a bit longer and try again. Either way, you need to be subtle to avoid it becoming a comedy routine or just plain creepy, thus alienating your client completely.

Once you have encouraged your client to open up to you and they have described things in their own words, you can go back and ask them to expand on anything they've said where you're not sure of their meaning, or need more information. This is called clarifying and for the client above you might ask 'What sort of bad things have made you go back to smoking in the past?' Or ' What do you mean by being stressed out?' If the client struggles to say more, asking for examples can be a good way into this: 'Tell me about one of the times you went back to smoking because of stress'.

Try this out: understand and clarify

Ask someone to describe something they feel emotional about, maybe a memory that has strong positive connections for them, or how annoyed they become if someone cuts in front of them when they are driving. Use active listening to encourage them to keep talking and make a note of any words or phrases you want to clarify at the end. Use paraphrasing, re-stating and the other feedback techniques mentioned to check with them that you have listened and understood how they feel.

To bring all this together then, active listening can be a great way to show the client you are interested in them and what they say, and you can do this by:

- Adopting a posture that shows interest
- Sitting at the right angle and distance from the client
- Using eye contact and other NVC
- Not allowing note-taking to become intrusive
- Avoiding noisy or distracting environments
- Ensuring the session is not interrupted by phones etc
- Avoiding physical barriers
- Being aware of your own NVC
- Remaining non-judgemental in your thoughts as well as your words
- Giving feedback without interrupting or imposing your own interpretation
- Offering subtle encouragements to continue – hmm, nods, facial expressions
- Allowing silences so the client can process what they want to say

- Using paraphrasing and restatement to confirm that you have understood, or for clarification
- Use feeling reflections to validate the client's experience
- Use pacing and leading of the other person's language patterns, NVC
- Clarify anything you're not sure of

Understanding your client's language

By this I don't mean whether your client is speaking English or Ancient Latin. It's more about the ways they choose to describe their issues to you and to themselves.

You are probably already aware that you process the world via your senses – sight, touch, hearing, smell and taste. Some situations prioritise one of these over another. Listening to a radio for example is done through the sense of hearing. Watching a film prioritises sight and hearing. Eating a meal can use all five senses.

As you go through life, you lay down memories, which are a kind of internal representation of where you have been and what you've experienced. These include not just events, but any emotions and perceptions that are connected to that event. We're not going to go into the biology of how that happens here, but we will say that we seem to encode and process this information mostly in terms of the five senses so that when we think about things, recall memories or use our imagination we do so, again, through our senses. 'Representational systems' or 'modalities' are the terms generally used to describe this.

Although we have five external senses, the three most commonly used internal representational systems are visual (processing in images), kinaesthetic (processing by feeling, which can mean either touch or emotion) and auditory (processing by sound).

Try this out: all your senses

Think about your favourite meal, or fish and chips at the seaside, or the smell of beer as you walk past a pub. For most people that brings about primarily a memory of smell or taste. Now imagine listening to your favourite music, looking at beautiful scenery or cupping your hands around a mug of tea on a cold day. You probably experienced these as sound, images or warmth because you can use your mind's 'internal senses' to create these experiences in just the same way you used your external ones to experience them in the first place.

Taste and smell tend to be reserved for recalling tastes and smells rather than for encoding other experiences and are therefore usually thought of as secondary representational systems. However where they are used they are referred to as gustatory (taste) and olfactory (smell).

There is another representational system too, known as digital. This refers to processing the world through words, logic and other 'non-sensory' means. Sometimes this is subdivided into auditory digital (processing language by imagining how it would sound) and visual digital (processing language by thinking about how it would look written down).

Interestingly, a small percentage of the population has a condition called synaesthesia which changes the ways in which they experience the world so, for example, musical notes might be experienced as colours, or words might be experienced as tastes.

This has been connected to differences in the way white matter is arranged in the brain and to the existence of more grey matter in some of the regions related to perception.[3]

Getting back to our main point, though, just as some of us have better eyesight or a better sense of smell than others, most of us find it easier to encode or retrieve thoughts in some representational systems than others. Perhaps you noticed this about yourself if you did the exercise in the box above. It's also why wedding dress shops, supermarkets, car salespeople, and the like try to use all our senses in their displays. In a therapy context, if you know how your client is processing their situation you can start to deal with it in those terms.

The next question of course, is how you can find this out, and there are thought to be a number of indicators we can use. You'll recall that we said much of our non-verbal communication was unconscious. These indicators are said to be the unconscious indicators of the representational systems a client is using in much the same way.

- **Language:** it is suggested that people's thinking preferences can unconsciously influence their choice of words, and particularly in the metaphors they use. For example, in describing their anxiety your client might say "I can't see a way out' (visual), or 'It's weighing me down' (kinaesthetic) or 'It all sounds like too much for me to cope with' (auditory). It would be unrealistic for just one of these phrases to be taken as a guide to someone's favoured representational systems. Common phrases like 'I see' are used by many people, visual or otherwise. But the repetition of many of these tiny clues in someone's conversation, especially in the ways in which they describe their problem, can indicate the way they are processing the issue they want you to deal with.
- **Eye accessing cues:** this is quite a controversial area, some people are very enthusiastic about it while others reject the

whole idea. In addition, some people seem to give much clearer eye accessing cues than others. The theory is that people who are visualising tend to look upwards, those who are thinking about a sound look to one side, and those who are thinking about a sensation (either physical or emotional) or words tend to look downwards. There are more detailed versions which suggest that whether someone is looking left or right indicates whether they are recalling or imagining auditory or visual experiences.

- **Jobs and hobbies:** a photographer is quite likely to be primarily visual; they can see the shot they want in their minds before they ever lift up a camera. A composer is likely to be auditory, a craftsman kinaesthetic (just think of that pottery scene in the film *Ghost*). Gardeners might be visual (if the look of the garden is most important to them) or kinaesthetic (if it's the feel of getting their hands in the dirt).
- **Learning styles:** how do you recall your bank PIN or phone number? Do you imagine seeing it written down? (Visual) Is there a word that reminds you of it? (Digital) Or hearing it spoken? (Auditory) Is it the shape of the movements needed to press the right keys? (Kinaesthetic)
- **Decision making:** if you are buying clothing, what matters most? Is it how it looks, either in your mind's eye or in a mirror? (Visual) Or do you need to touch the material, move around in it to see how it feels? (Kinaesthetic)

it is possible to use a questionnaire to identify your client's preferred representational system. These are freely available online, just carry out a search, and they are quite interesting. However they can take up quite a bit of time in your session and they work with generalities. Even if your client generally prefers to think kinaesthetically, she may be processing the issue which brought her to see you another way. Once you have an idea of what representational system your client is working in then you can use this to create session content that is meaningful and comfortable for them. We'll come back to this when we talk about adapting scripts but we can also use it in the pre-talk. If your client describes her anxiety kinaesthetically by saying it's weighing her down, responding in the same system by saying something like: 'What would it take to make it lighter?' is better than making a visual comment such as 'What would help you see things differently?'

Absolutes and other words to watch for

Most clients have lived with their problem for a while before they arrive in your office. They have talked it over with family, friends, a GP or even other therapists. They will have developed a point of view, and perhaps even favourite ways of describing things, and they will tell you about their situation in those terms. As you listen, pick out those places where your clients' thinking processes might be getting in the way of progress because that is what can give you a place to begin their therapy.

Do you recall our smoking client who said she can quit for a week or so but . . . it never lasts? As long as she believes that, it arguably never will last because we all tend to treat our beliefs as if they are facts. And if it's a fact that it never lasts, then it is pointless her even trying to quit. This kind of statement or generalisation will give you a place to begin your therapy, because if we can reframe or dismantle that belief we can move forwards. These are the kind of things to listen out for:

- Avoidance: I don't want to talk about my parents; they have nothing to do with this.
- Assumptions: I don't need to tell them how I feel, they already know.

- Incomplete information: It just is. You know what I mean.
- Generalisations: Nothing ever changes. I always do the wrong thing.
- Absolutes and unrealistic expectations: My life is over if I don't pass this exam. He must show more respect for me.

Chapter summary

'In my early professional years I was asking the question: How can I treat, or cure, or change this person? Now I would phrase the question in this way: How can I provide a relationship which this person may use for his own personal growth'
Carl Rogers
(www.brainyquote.com/quotes/quotes/c/carlrogers202206.html)

In other words, if you can get into your client's world and build a relationship that allows them to feel safe, you can help them find the coping strategies and solutions that are right for them instead of imposing your own ideas.
Ways into the client's world include:

- building rapport through empathy
- being aware of all aspects of the client's NVC and your own: visual, tactile, vocal and use of time, space and images
- using active listening
- listening to the way people express themselves as well as what they are expressing and responding in appropriate ways
- listening for clues about any barriers to progress perceived by the client

References and Notes

1. Wertheim, Edward G. Ph.D *The Importance of Effective Communication*, Northeastern University, College of Business Administration, retrieved 10/10/08 from http://web.cba.neu.edu/~ewertheim/interper/commun.htm [accessed May 2016]

2. Mehrabian, Albert (2009). ""Silent Messages" – A Wealth of Information About Nonverbal Communication (Body Language)". in *Personality & Emotion Tests & Software: Psychological Books & Articles of Popular Interest*. Los Angeles, CA: self-published.

3. Rouw & Schulte, 2007, cited in *Synaesthesia Research*, University of Sussex, http://www.sussex.ac.uk/synaesthesia/faq [accessed May 2016]

Chapter Two

Exploring your client's world

If you are going to change your client's world you need to understand it deeply and profoundly. Here we look at some ways you can develop this understanding.

We've discussed how you can build rapport and enter into your client's point of view, so you can understand as exactly as possible how they experience their world.

This has involved both observation and listening, along with some brief responses you might make to keep your client talking. But sometimes offering encouragement and reflecting back what the client has said is not enough; we need to ask for more information, start a new topic, or guide the client back to the subject at hand. We're looking now at the best ways to do this.

Clean Language

In a therapeutic setting, clean language doesn't mean not swearing (although you should probably keep your language clean in that sense too!). Using clean language means avoiding leading questions, which are those that suggest a specific answer. For example, asking your client: ‘Do you feel anxious when that happens?' would probably lead them to say 'Yes' as long as anxiety was somewhere in the right area. But asking specifically about anxiety reflects what you suppose the client feels, and not their own experience. When we're trying to get right into the client's world and see things from their point of view, we need their own descriptors.

A non-leading question such as ‘How do you feel when that happens?' might mean the client replies 'Anxious', but it could also be scared, apprehensive or something else entirely. Using the right words matters.

The concept of clean language was developed by therapist David Grove in the 1980's but it's now used in a wide variety of situations; you will be familiar with it if you watch police or courtroom dramas on TV. ‘Tell me how you killed your wife’ presupposes that you did, and would bring the defence leaping to their feet with an objection.

In a therapy setting, clean language is used to keep your own ideas and assumptions out of the way when you are talking to clients.

Let's look at another example. A client says, ‘I'm stuck in this terrible marriage and I can’t see a way out.' If you respond, ‘What would give you the courage to walk away?' you are not using 'clean' language. It imposes your view of the answer (walking away) and assumes that courage is what the client needs to achieve it. A clean response would be ‘What would need to happen for that to change?' or 'Is there anything else you can tell me about being stuck?'

Clean language is essential in every part of your therapy session, in and out of hypnosis, because it means you allow the client to tell their own story in their own way. In fact,

Try this out: clean alternatives

Think of a clean language alternative for each of these questions.
Do you smoke more when you're stressed?
Did you feel sad about that?
Is that when you lost your temper?
Did you think he was going to hit you?

Try this out: story outline

Ask someone to tell you the brief outline of a story and practise clean language questions to fill in the details. If they are not sure what to talk about, role playing a fictional character can work well - Cinderella talking about how she wants to go to a party but has lost confidence in social situations recently, for example.

not using clean language is generally thought to be the basis of 'false memory syndrome', a term which refers to memories which have been brought about by careless or leading questions. The memories have no foundation in fact, and no evidence to support them, but the client can come to believe they are true.

This might seem implausible but think how real a dream, or even your client's peaceful place, can feel. In trance your client is very open to suggestion, that's exactly why hypnotherapy works. An implicit suggestion, during a regression perhaps, that an event took place, or that it took place in a particular way, combined with the fact that the unconscious is largely unable to distinguish between reality and imagination, does the rest.

If you ever find yourself in a session where you not sure how to respond to something the client says, questions like 'What happened next?', 'Can you tell me more about that?', 'Why do you think that was?' or 'How did that make you feel?' will usually get the conversation going again.

How to ask for information: Brown's Question Cube[1]

There are many different kinds of questions, and as therapists we need to be aware of the sort of information each of them is likely to obtain for us. We need to understand the client's situation, which may be quite complex, and to get as much relevant information as possible within the time limitations of our appointment with them.

Jacob Brown developed a system he called the 'Question Cube' (because it is three-dimensional) for use by trainee couple and family therapists, but it suits our purposes as hypnotherapists very well.

The three dimensions he identified are *format, subject* and *orientation*, so let's look at each of these in turn.

Question format

This is the way you structure your questions in order to get the kind of information that's useful to you in helping the client. You will probably use all of the formats at different times.

- *Open question*: this invites more information without specifying what kind of information is required. It's great for finding out about your client but can lead to lots of extraneous details for you to sort through. An example would be: 'Why do you think you are still smoking?'

• *Closed question*: this invites a brief or very specific reply, most useful when we want very practical information. It's nonsensical to ask an open question like 'What can you tell me about your phone?' if all you want is the number. Closed questions are less useful when we're exploring motivations or beliefs: 'Are you still smoking now because of stress?' is not only a leading question, it's a closed one likely to result in a yes or no answer. This, firstly, is not very informative and, secondly, may mean the client does not get the chance to give you information about other relevant factors like socialising.
• *Forced-choice question:* ones which give a limited choice of answers. 'Did you buy this book to improve your skills as a hypnotherapist or to prop up the wobbly leg on your desk?' These are useful for clarifying or encouraging a client who is shy, or reluctant to share information, or who is not really in touch with their feelings. In these circumstances 'Do you think what you're feeling is fear, or anger?' can be easier to answer than an open question like 'How does that make you feel?' However, we must be careful with forced-choice questions so as not to lead the client, and they can restrict someone for whom none of the suggested answers is appropriate. A good way to deal with this is to offer the client the option of adding their own answer, for example 'Do you think being overweight is down to eating too much, or eating the wrong things, or something else?'
• *Ranking question:* this asks the client to place things in order of importance. Ranking questions are very useful for checking the client's motivations and priorities. For example, your client says they want to stop smoking so they can use the money to put their kids through college, but they worry that quitting will be difficult because all their friends still smoke. You could ask 'Is it more important to you to help

Try this out: open and closed

Ask someone about their hobby, using the different kinds of questions listed. Count how many of each type you use. Do the same thing again and deliberately change the balance, so you are asking more open questions. (If your questions were mostly open anyway, try changing to more closed ones instead.) What difference does this make to the information you get?

your children, or to be like your friends?'

- *Rating questions:* these are very similar to ranking but also ask the client to evaluate their answers, once characteristics have been ranked. 'How much more important is it to help your children than to be like your friends?' Using a SUDS (Subjective Units of Distress) scale is a useful way to do this, giving each option a mark out of ten.

Question subject

Brown identifies five areas in which we can explore the client's experiences; they are how we start to identify what we want to know. Generally speaking, we would start at the top of the list and work down, because behaviour questions are often the easiest for the client to answer.

- Behaviours: 'What did you do?'
- Feelings: 'How did that make you feel?'
- Beliefs/thoughts: 'Why do you think you do that?' 'What makes that happen?'
- Meaning: 'You say you want to be 'normal', what would that be like?'
- Relationships: 'How is that important to what's brought

you here today?'

We have already said that Brown was developing a model for trainees who intended to work in couples or family counselling, and in that context 'relationships' tended to mean the relationships of the people within the family or therapy group. However, we can quite reasonably broaden this to mean all kinds of relationships, not just with other people, but with other elements of the client's life as well.

Question Orientation

Finally, Brown suggested we should think about the orientation of the questions, in other words whether we are asking about the client or someone else. This perhaps highlights the origins of the model in couples/family therapy, but it is perfectly relevant for you to ask about how the client's situation affects others in their social circles.

- Questions seeking the client's perspective (self-

> ### *Try this out: place the questions*
>
> **Place these questions into the three categories as I have done with the one on the next page: (my answers are at the end of the chapter)**
>
> **How many cigarettes do you smoke a day?**
>
> **How do your family feel about your smoking?**
>
> **Why do you think cigarettes help when you are stressed?**
>
> **Do you want to reduce the amount you smoke, or stop altogether?**
>
> **How will you recognise 'healthier'?**

orientation): 'How do you feel about your smoking?'

- Questions seeking their view of another person's perspective (other orientation): 'How do you think your partner feels about your smoking?'

Questioning skills and active listening

According to Brown, questions can be placed into all three categories, so for example that last one ('How do you think your partner feels about your smoking?') is open/beliefs/other.

You've probably heard that ASSUME makes an ASS out of U and ME. Questioning skills should always be used alongside active listening, and you should never assume that you have understood your client. Always paraphrase, restate, and clarify to make sure.

Clients who 'don't know' the answer

Although clean language and open questions are a good way to get information from your client without influencing them, it can be difficult to respond if they frequently answer: 'I don't know'. It's very tempting at these times to leap in and offer some of your own solutions, but this can undermine your client's autonomy and result in a less accurate understanding of their world.

There is, of course, no single correct way to deal with this answer because there is no single reason clients give it, but there are responses that might help things move on.

- Leave a period of silence, your client may take the opportunity to think about it some more and elaborate.
- Ask the client to come up with a solution to not knowing. 'How could you find out?', 'If you had to guess the answer, what might it be?' or 'What would need to be different for you to know that?'

- Encourage the client to look at things from another perspective, asking questions like: 'What do you think someone else would say to that?' or 'How would you advise your best friend if they were in this situation?'
- Use re-stating, your client knows what they mean even if they can't explain it.
- If the client is having trouble finding the right words, offer different ways to express the answer such as drawing, writing it down or creating a metaphor.
- Ask the client if they know what the answer definitely isn't. Sometimes ruling things out can be a good place to start.
- Ask them to close their eyes and take a couple of deep breaths, imagine themselves in the relevant situation and become aware of the answers.
- Use content-free techniques if you know them.
- Ask the client if they can select one of a number of choices, for example, 'When they get cravings some of my other clients have found it useful to drink water, do number puzzles, go for a walk or ring a friend. Do you think any of those options might be helpful for you?'
- Ask your client to brainstorm as many possible answers as they can in a short time limit, say two or three minutes. Write down everything they think of even if it's completely silly or impossible. After the time limit, go through the list and see if there are any ideas that might be useful.

Checking your own approach

- Ensure you have a good level of rapport, so your client feels they can tell you anything without being judged.
- Check that you are giving your clients enough time to process the questions you ask.
- Consider other issues which might be affecting the

situation: clients with trust issues may be reluctant to share personal information, clients with low self esteem may worry about being criticised, clients with strong secondary gain or low motivation may unconsciously block your attempts to help them.

- Remember that although your job is not to offer answers, you can teach skills like calm breathing, and coping strategies such as anchors and triggers, which may become answers.

Structuring the session: T.H.E.R.A.P.Y.

Once you have basic information about your client, their situation and what they want you to deal with, you will need to pick up on aspects of what they've said to find out more.

So far in this chapter, we've looked at the general areas you might like to ask your clients about, but many inexperienced therapists (and some more experienced ones) wonder how to structure their intake interview to get all the information they need.

The simplest way to gather the information you need is to design an intake form. You could give this form to the client to complete at or before the first appointment, or fill it in yourself as you chat.

Your form will definitely need to include:

- the client's name and contact details
- their preferred method of contact in case you need to get in touch between sessions. (If this is phone, ask if anyone else ever answers it; if yes, check whether it's OK to leave messages. Even if the client says you can, stick to your name and number and 'Please call me back', to preserve confidentiality.)
- brief medical history and any current medications (to

check for contraindications or other possible causes of the problem)

You could also include:

- their age (if you feel it's relevant)
- family situation
- job, hobbies/interests, and other information that might help you identify their preferred representational systems
- a place they would like to go to in their minds to relax (so you can build a peaceful place)
- if there are any phobias not related to their presenting problem, or situations you should avoid when using imagery or metaphor techniques (water, heights, small spaces, etc.)
- lifestyle questions such as whether or how much they drink or smoke, whether they follow a healthy diet and take regular exercise, whether they feel they get enough sleep
- any significant events such as bereavements, house moves, family changes and the like that have occurred in the last 12 months. Even if they are not obviously connected to the presenting issue, they might impact on the client's coping abilities
- any history of trauma, for example bullying or abuse
- if they have had hypnotherapy before; if they have, ask when, what for, and how successful it was
- where the client first saw your name (to support your marketing)

I strongly suggest that you also have a written terms and conditions sheet or contract setting out the way in which you work, along with both your and the client's rights and responsibilities. Ask the client to sign a copy.

You then have to ask about why they have come to therapy, and of course you'll want to use all of the skills we have covered so far in doing this. To give this part of the discussion some structure, I recommend remembering the word THERAPY. In this instance it's an acronym, which means that each letter can remind you of something you need to ask or do. Briefly they stand for:

- **T**est the goals
- **H**istory to here and now
- **E**stablish what needs to change
- **R**e-imagine the future
- **A**dd-ons and aggravations
- **P**lanning
- **Y**omp ahead

Let's look at each of these in turn.

Testing the goals

Most clients arrive with a goal in mind but they might not be very precise. It's going to be easier for you to aim your hypnotherapy suggestions at something which has plenty of detail and specifics, so you may need to tweak their original goal into a more useful format. There are the three main criteria to help you test the goal.

1. Goals should be positive, in other words they should state what the client wants and not what they don't want.
2. Goals should be SMART (specific, measurable, achievable, relevant and time-bound) see Appendix One if this is not a familiar concept to you.
3. Can the goal be reached in one step, or do you need to break it down into smaller ones to make it more manageable?

Let's see how this works in practice. A client comes to you wishing to work with insomnia, they tell you their goal is to avoid spending two or more hours trying to get to sleep every night.

Test 1. this is a negative, focused on what they want to

avoid. If we ask the client to say what they do want instead, they might say 'a good night's sleep'.

Test 2. the goal is now positive but still a bit vague. What is a good night's sleep? By using clean language and establishing what this means to the client we could come up with something SMARTer like 'Within two months I want to fall sleep within 15 minutes of switching the light off, and sleep without waking for at least six hours'. Making a goal positive can be done right at the beginning of the session but if your client's goal is not initially SMART, it may be easier to re-word it after you have collected more information.

Test 3. It's unlikely that anyone would move from taking two hours to fall asleep to 15 minutes in one step. A far more realistic scenario is a gradual improvement. Setting interim goals would work with this, and it might also be useful to split the main goal into (a) time taken to fall asleep and (b) how long the client sleeps without waking. Splitting goals like this is often called 'chunking them down'.

***H**istory to **H**ere and Now*

This is often the longest part of the intake, where you explore those parts of the client's world that relate to the issue they have come to see you about. Most people start

Try this out: talk to a volunteer

about a feeling or behaviour they'd like to change (it can be real or imagined for the sake of the exercise). Use the T.H.E.R.A.P.Y. approach to gather information about it and come up with a therapy plan.

by giving you a brief statement, for example ‘My partner and I want to start a family, so I'm here for help to stop smoking.' From that initial point, you need to ask about:

1. The here and now: how their issue affects them on a day-to-day basis, what difficulties it causes for them, what benefits (if any) it might provide, how it feels to have this problem, and what has made them choose right now to change it. This last one is important given that there is generally a catalyst for the client to seek out a change when they haven’t done so before. One of my clients, for example, had lived with a public speaking phobia for years but finally decided to deal with it when she was promoted to a job which included giving regular presentations.
2. The history: how long has the problem been around, have there been changes in intensity; if so, what brought these about, has the client already tried to change things; if so, what did they do and how well did it work, if not, why do they feel it didn't work, and so on.

'W' questions are generally a good place to start: who, what, why, when, where? (Also how, even though it’s not a W.)

Aim to cover the five areas identified by Brown as ‘question subjects', starting with the behaviours, feelings or beliefs which are involved with their issue. Don’t forget to include questions about how other people who are important to them might be affected (either by the status quo or by a change in it), and how the presenting problem relates to other areas of their lives.

***E**stablish what needs to change*

This should follow on quite naturally from talking about therapy goals and the client's ‘here and now'. The client may not know exactly how to change , that's why they have come to see you, but they will almost certainly have an idea of what needs to be different. What you need to know is how they see that happening, the process of change if you like. What do they hope hypnotherapy can provide for them that they haven't got now? Is it realistic for you to provide that? If not, is it a matter of reconsidering the goals or referring the client to someone more experienced?

***Re**-imagine the future*

How does your client see the future, once they have reached their goal? What will the benefits of making this change be for them and what will be better?

In some circumstances you might also want to ask how the client sees the future if they don't achieve their goals. This can uncover some of the motivators that have caused them to seek out therapy, and also any worries or concerns they might have about making significant changes.

In either case, you need as much detail as possible, so:

1. Use as many as possible of the sensory modalities to describe their future self: what do they see, hear, touch, taste, smell?
2. Cover all of Brown's subject areas: what will they do, what feelings will they experience, will any of their beliefs have changed? Will this change affect others? If so, how? Will there be a knock-on effect in other areas of their lives?

***A**dd-ons and **A**ggravations*

By now you have a lot of information: where the client wants to be, how far from that they are now, how they are going to get there, and what it will be like when they do. Now take a moment or two to check wider issues.

Add-ons are those things the client is going to do to extend or support the therapy you will do together, in other words homework. This could be as simple as listening to your CD every night, or getting some physical symptoms checked out by their GP. Or it could be more challenging, such as going outside their comfort zone to test how well your work together is going.

Aggravations are things that get in the way of a smooth progression. Some can be predicted, like our smoking client from Chapter One who says she always returns to smoking when she's stressed. You might be able to pre-empt this type of difficulty, teaching your client stress management techniques would be useful, or asking her to practise relaxation techniques daily. Some aggravations, like a work emergency or sick child, may prevent the client from completing their homework but cannot be predicted. When this happens, you'll need to review suitable coping strategies as you go.

__P__lanning

At this stage you should be able to put together a therapy plan, although how formal or detailed this is will depend on how you prefer to work, and the techniques you favour. Remember, though, that whatever your approach, few therapy plans remain unchanged through the whole course of therapy and you should not stick slavishly to them, no matter what happens. Flexibility is the key to providing effective, personalised session content.

__Y__omp ahead

Yomp is Royal Marines slang for a march over challenging terrain carrying full kit, it's thought to be an acronym for Your Own Marching Pace. I've chosen it because it works really well as a metaphor for providing therapy. Once you have all the information you need, and a plan, the final step is for you and your client to shoulder their 'baggage' and travel together at their 'own pace' across whatever terrain you find in their world, until you reach your goal.

Second and subsequent sessions

Most of our attention so far has been on the first session because that's where you gather the initial information about your client. However, you can continue to use T.H.E.R.A.P.Y. in later sessions.

- Test the goals. Have they changed? Or been achieved?
- Here and now. In what ways is the client's reality different? Or the same?
- Establish what (still) needs to change. How well is the therapy working so far? What do you still need to address or improve?
- Re-imagine the future. As they move towards their goals, is their reality the way they expected it to be? If not, how is it different?
- Add-ons and Aggravations. Have they carried out any agreed tasks? If not, why not? How can you prevent this being a problem next time? Are there any new add-ons or aggravations to consider?
- Planning. Do you need to update your therapy plan, or are you still on track?
- Yomp ahead. Moving on towards your goal, in other words providing the therapy for this session.

Summarising

As you'll have realised by now, you have a lot of information to gather to provide personalised and effective therapy. Both you and the client will have a lot to process by the end of the session, so to keep you on track and firmly in the client's world we come finally to summarising.

This means giving a little word-picture of what has happened so far, and is useful to provide structure and to link between one part of the session and another. It should be fairly brief but cover the most important points.

For example, once you have completed your initial chat, it's wise to summarise your understanding of why the client has come to see you and what they want to achieve from their work with you before you move on to providing any therapy. So you could say something like:

'So, your goal is to lose one stone by the time you get married in three months. You find it easy to eat healthy food at mealtimes, but you tend to snack on biscuits and chocolate when you are watching TV alone in the evenings. We've decided you would prefer to have a drink of water or a piece of fruit at those times, and we'll reinforce that choice in the hypnosis part of the session. Does that sound right?'

It's essential to summarise what's been achieved at the end of each session as well, so the client goes away feeling that you've progressed. It's also a perfect chance to check that you and the client agree about how things are going. Here is an example of this:

'Today we started by talking about your snacking, and found out that it was linked to stress and feeling abandoned when your partner goes away to work.

'We used hypnosis to help reduce your stress and reinforce healthier choices, and next week we're going to explore why your partner being away might be difficult for you. You're going to keep a mood diary between now and then, so we can see if there are any other triggers to that feeling.

'Is there anything you would like to add, or ask about that before we finish?'

Chapter Summary

"It's not too difficult to get the skeletons out of the closet with people, but to get the gold out is a different matter. That is therapy."
Robert A Johnson
(www.psychology.wikia.com/wiki/Robert_A._Johnson)

If you want to help the client change their world, you need to understand it as it is now as thoroughly as possible. That means asking questions which are going to get you the information you need. Brown's Question Cube identifies what you need to ask about in general terms:

- behaviour
- feelings
- beliefs
- meanings
- relationships

It also helps you think about the ways in which you can phrase your questions to get the right level of information. The T.H.E.R.A.P.Y. protocol provides a framework within which to ask these questions. It ensures that you've taken a full 360-degree look at the client's world, so you know where they want to be, where they are and have been, what might help or hinder them on that journey, and how you can help.
So, now that you have all that information, let's look at how you can use it to provide effective hypnotherapy.

References and notes

1. Brown, J. E. (1997). The question cube: a model for developing question repertoire in training couple and family therapists. *Journal of Marital and Family Therapy, 23*(1), 27–40.

Question Cube exercise:

How many cigarettes do you smoke a day? *Closed/behaviour/self*

How do your family feel about your smoking? *Open/feelings/other*

Why do you think cigarettes help when you are stressed? *Open/belief/self*

Do you want to reduce the amount you smoke or stop altogether? *Forced choice/behaviour/self*

How will you recognise 'healthier'? *Open/meaning/self*

Chapter Three

Changing your client's world

The point of therapy is to help your client make positive changes. Here we look at techniques for doing this which use your client's ways of understanding the world.

Having talked about how you can build a relationship with your clients, and collect the right information from them, we are changing our direction a bit and going on to look at how you can start to move things on. In order to do this, we're going to define a couple of basic concepts, such as 'therapy' and 'suggestion', and then look at how you can use these to help your clients.

These clients come to you because there is something in their world they want to change. Some already know what the answer is. A weight control client, for example, may be aware that eating less and exercising more will get them to their ideal healthy body weight, but they need your help to achieve that. Other clients may have little or no idea what will work for them, and then you'll need to help them identify the right solutions as well as to put them in place.

Either way, your job as a therapist is not to have a series

of 'off the shelf' answers at your fingertips. Just as your clients' worlds are different, their solutions may be too. Your role is one of facilitation and empowerment, rather than manipulation and control, so the goal of really effective therapy is find the changes that are helpful — and practical — for each individual client.

What do we mean by 'therapy'?

I'm going to define therapy fairly broadly as 'any technique or procedure which is intended to help someone make a positive change, solve a personal problem or improve their well-being'. Within most talking therapies, coaching and counselling for example, there is no clear demarcation between asking the client for information and offering therapy, as talking to your client *is* the therapy. Within hypnotherapy, clients — and some therapists! — seem to separate the 'talking part' (what we've covered in this book so far) from the 'therapy part' (the hypnosis).

This, of course, isn't a realistic separation, as plenty of 'therapy' goes on outside trance, whether or not your client recognises it as such. You can teach controlled breathing and other coping strategies, or plan activities such as keeping a thought diary. Some techniques, such as anchoring, can be used in or out of trance, as can hypnotic language. Simply by listening to your client and responding in the right way you can help them understand patterns in their thinking and behaviour, and begin to change some of their ideas. This is usually called 'reframing' and the approach is not to challenge the client's way of thinking directly, which might break rapport, but to give them an opening through which they can challenge it for themselves.

For example, one of my clients told me about an occasion when he'd done something which had hurt others. He generally thought of himself as a kind and ethical person, and this memory of a time when he felt he'd been neither was still upsetting him 30 years later. Intellectually he accepted that there were extenuating circumstances, that he hadn't seen any other course of action at the time, and that he'd done what he could to put things right afterwards, but he didn't make any allowances for this emotionally. In his world, that one moment overruled all the evidence that hurting others wasn't his typical behaviour. I asked: 'If someone else did the same thing in the same circumstances, would you judge them as harshly as you're judging yourself?' After thinking about it for a while, he realised that he wouldn't, and that simple question was the beginning of a big change for him. He could start to use his tolerance and understanding on himself. Merely telling him that he shouldn't judge himself was unlikely to have had the same effect.

The power of suggestion

We'll look in a moment at how we can make therapeutic suggestions as powerful as possible, but first we have to decide what a suggestion actually is. www.dictionary.reference.com[1] offers a number of definitions for the word including:

1. something suggested as a piece of advice: 'We made the suggestion that she resign.'
2. the calling up in the mind of one idea by another, by virtue of some association or of some natural connection between the ideas.

In everyday life this is the difference between saying to someone, 'Why don't you get me a cup of tea?' (the first option) and 'I'm dying for a cup of tea' or even 'Are you as thirsty as I am?' (the second). One approach might be a bit more subtle than the other, but hopefully both have the desired effect of getting someone else to make you a drink.

As hypnotherapists we work on the assumption that hypnosis somehow changes or enhances the way people respond to suggestions, making them more likely to respond, and there is some evidence to support this idea.

David Spiegel, MD, of Stanford University, carried out a study which used PET scans to monitor how the brains of study participants responded to suggestion.[2] Half the participants were hypnotised, half were not. Both groups were shown patchwork images, some of which were coloured and some of which were greyscale. Suggestions were given with each image that the participant should visualise it in colour or black and white.

Different areas of the brain are involved in processing coloured and monochrome images and, for those in hypnosis, the activated areas depended on what they were asked to visualise, regardless of whether it matched the image they were looking at. For example, if they were asked to look at a greyscale image, but to imagine it in colour, the colour-processing parts of the brain became active.

For those not in hypnosis, the colour-processing areas

Try this out: identify language patterns

Listen out for language patterns in people who want others to do something for them. Which of these are they using? What do you think gets the best results?

were only active when they looked at colour images, although some other areas of the brain did seem to react to the image more in line with the suggestions than reality.

Spiegel (ibid.) concluded that: "...with hypnosis, we can help people modulate perceptions in ways that are therapeutically helpful."

Of course, the other way of looking at this is that even those who were not in hypnosis followed the suggestion to imagine the images in different ways. The truth is that we are all suggestible, whether we're in hypnosis or not, and it doesn't seem to matter whether the suggestion is given to us directly or obliquely. This is one reason we included the use of time, for example, in our discussion of non-verbal communication. Keeping someone waiting for hours creates a powerful suggestion that their time is not as valuable as yours.

Robert Michael, from the Victoria University of Wellington, New Zealand, says:

"We encounter suggestion every day of our lives. We like to believe that our thoughts and our behaviours are rationally constructed, but what the research shows is that, in fact, our thoughts and our behaviours are influenced by all manner of seemingly irrelevant information — including suggestion and expectation." [3]

Of course, exactly how suggestible we are varies from one situation to another, and also between individuals. Even so, Wilson (2011) says that "there is considerable scientific support for [using] the power of suggestion within a therapeutic setting." [4]

Although we are going on to look at the way suggestions are crafted for the trance part of your session, this is a really important point. Wilson is not talking about hypnosis at all, and you can use suggestion-based language both in and out of trance to help your clients get the most from your sessions.

Creating effective therapeutic suggestions

Styles of suggestion:

We started the last section with two different definitions of suggestion, one quite straightforward, almost an instruction, and one more implied. These tally quite well with what hypnotherapists refer to as direct and indirect suggestion.

We've already said that within a therapy session it is not your job to give advice or instructions to your client, so you might assume that therapeutic suggestions should be closer to the second, indirect style. This isn't necessarily the case, though.

Suppose you asked your client to imagine walking along a corridor and arriving at a door. You want them to give you some indication when they've done this, so you say, "When you've done this, give me a nod." In this context, a direct suggestion simply makes more sense than an indirect one.

Direct suggestions can also be useful if a client comes to you with a specific solution to their problem already in mind, or if you have agreed a coping strategy in your pre-talk. For example, your client decides that they want to embark on a healthy eating regime designed to promote general fitness and weight reduction. As part of this, they want to replace their current habit of snacking on crisps with drinking water. In this case you might say something like:

"From now on, when you sit down in the evening you sip a glass of cool, fresh water. When you do this you feel completely satisfied in every way: emotionally, physically and psychologically. You feel amazing whenever you reject crisps, or any other unhealthy, fatty or salty snacks. You respect your health, you enjoy sipping cool, fresh water and you absolutely refuse to allow junk food into your body."

This is of course very specific and direct, but it's acceptable because you are not imposing your own advice or solutions. You are simply reinforcing the client's choice, or their own good advice to themselves.

If the same client arrives knowing that they want to stop eating so many crisps but not knowing how, or can't settle on a suitable replacement activity, you should not unilaterally decide that they need to drink water instead of eating crisps. In this case it's best to use a more indirect approach, such as:

"As you sit down in the evening, your imagination and your wonderful, creative unconscious mind finds more and more ways to replace the old unhealthy habits with new healthy ones. You feel amazing whenever you make positive, healthy choices, you know you are taking control of your eating habits and allowing your body to become fit and slim. Each time you see your reflection you feel a growing sense of satisfaction that your body is healthy and strong, you treat your body in the way you know it deserves . . ."

As you'll see, this doesn't suggest any specific replacement activity for the crisps, but by associating the ideas of new healthy habits with positive feelings it encourages the client to find their own best solutions. That might even turn out to be drinking more water, but the client is given the choice.

As we're aiming to work within our client's world, it shouldn't come as too much of a surprise to know that your client's personality and experience, too, can shape your choice of suggestions. A client who enjoys structure and certainty may feel more at home with a direct suggestion than with an indirect approach, because the expected outcomes are more clear-cut: a client who dislikes authority figures or prefers to feel in control may find that a direct approach simply presses the 'rebel' button and encourages them to reject your suggestions.

In reality, of course, most sessions will include a mixture of the two, but you should get a sense of what will work best with your client as you explore their world. Just as their language patterns, job and hobbies can indicate their sensory processing preferences, they can also give clues to

Try this out: working with suggestions

Annie has come to you for help to quit smoking. She and her partner are planning to start a family and she does not want to smoke while pregnant. The money she saves by not buying cigarettes will also be useful, and she plans to put it aside to help cover expenses while she's on maternity leave. She feels she will miss the smoking most in the car; she travels a lot for work and smokes to relieve the boredom of driving.

(a) assume Annie hasn't been able to decide on any specific replacement activities or coping strategies to use at the times she used to smoke and write some indirect suggestions for her session

(b) assume Annie has chosen to use breathing exercises and low calorie chewing gum as replacement activities and write some direct suggestions to reinforce using these as coping strategies

whether they are likely to prefer the direct or indirect approach. An example often quoted is that someone in the military or another hierarchical career will tend to prefer more structured and direct suggestions, whereas creative 'free thinker' types might prefer indirect suggestion. Be careful of generalisations though. If your military client is a Major General and more used to giving orders than taking them, you might need to rethink.

Developing suggestion-based session content

There are a few guidelines to follow when creating therapeutic suggestions in any format to make them as effective as possible.

1. Use the present tense.

'You are calm and relaxed' instead of 'You will be calm and relaxed'.

'Will be' allows the suggestion to be accepted but not acted on, because it is vague about when or how quickly things should change. Use the present tense even when referring to future events, for example: 'When you walk into the exam room on Monday you are calm and relaxed.'

2. Be positive.

'You are calm and relaxed' instead of 'You are not anxious anymore.'

Negatives can simply remind a client of what they are trying to avoid. Create a vivid word picture of what the client *does* want to engage their emotions, imagination and unconscious ability to create it.

3. Use negatives in a positive way.

If you need to mention something your client no longer wants to do or think, associate it with taking positive, preventative action, for example: 'You reject cigarettes', 'You refuse to allow junk food into your life.'

4. Be detailed.

Saying: 'You enjoy playing football in the park with little Johnny, your breath coming easily, your lungs healthy, full of energy in mind and body,' is better than saying 'You feel healthier as a non-smoker.' This means making sure you get lots of details when you ask the client to 're-imagine' their future. If you ask: 'What will be better as a non-smoker?' many people will say something general like 'My health.' Ask them to imagine exactly what will be different and what effect this will have on their lives.

5. Be simple and straightforward.

Faced with a therapist saying: 'You extrapolate this positivism into a multiplicity of environments,' most clients would be confused. Much better to say: 'You take this confidence with you wherever you go.' You can work with complex ideas, of course, but do so in language that the client can follow.

Try this out: Use new information

Look back at the direct and indirect suggestions you wrote for Annie. Can you improve them now you have more information?

Try this out: Advertising and media

Pay attention to advertising you see online, in print media and on the television. Which of these guidelines do you notice being applied?

6. Be realistic.
If you are working with a client who has just started running say something like: 'You enjoy running more and more, feeling exhilarated whenever you improve your time.' instead of 'Imagine being offered a place in the Olympic team'.
6. Focus on elements which are under the client's control.
'You are calm, relaxed and focused in your interview, performing at your best,' instead of 'You will definitely get the job,' or 'You are the best candidate for the job'. Essentially, don't make promises that you, or the client, may not be able to keep!
7. 'But' undermines everything that went before it.
'I love your new hair style, but . . .' is never going to be followed by a compliment! This word should be used with care, and only where you intend to cancel out ideas: 'You used to be a smoker like them, but now you are free.'
8. Link one idea to another, if it is appropriate
- Where the client has identified relationships between what they want and how they want to feel: 'As you choose to enjoy this fresh, healthy food and your weight continues to reduce, you find yourself creating powerful feelings of happiness and confidence.'
- Where you have feedback from the client on how they experienced trance, perhaps from an earlier session with you: 'And as the sounds in the room fade into the background you can allow your fear of spiders to fade with them, drifting it into the past so that it no longer exists in your present or future . . .'

9. Use repetition.
The unconscious is more likely to accept ideas which are repeated, so choose a small number of linked changes and make suggestions which are variations on that theme,

rather than bombarding your client with a 'shopping list' of competing demands in one session.

More techniques to make your suggestions effective

Double binds: this is where you appear to give the client a choice but in fact whatever choice they make the result will be the same. For example:

"When you go to the garage to fill your car with petrol you may choose to not even notice the sweets and chocolates that used to be such a temptation. Or perhaps you will notice them, only to discover a feeling of pride and confidence that they no longer hold any attraction for you at all."

Embedded commands: this is where you appear to be using indirect or permissive language, but the emphasis you put on the words as you say them brings out the hidden commands. For example: 'You may find yourself relaxing now.' Read that out loud in a soothing tone and let it flow. It's gentle and permissive, apparently giving the client a choice. Now read it out again, putting a slight pause between the word 'may' and the word 'relaxing', and put a bit more emphasis on the final phrase: 'You may . . . find yourself relaxing now.' That final phrase is now an instruction.

Yes sets: essentially this is a form of pacing and leading. You offer several statements or questions where the client is sure to agree with you, then add another that you want them to agree with. For example: "You had the motivation to phone me and arrange this appointment, and you had the motivation to arrive on time . . . you had the motivation to listen to my voice as you relaxed on that chair, and you have all the motivation you need to be your ideal, healthy size and shape."

Confusional language: this is language designed so that the client's conscious mind may not be sure exactly what it is you're suggesting, but that we trust that the unconscious mind will understand. For example:

"It may be that you'll simply forget to remember that this was a time you used to overeat, or perhaps you'll only remember to forget it."

Reframing: reframing is essentially asking the client to view something in a different, more positive way. Simply saying, 'Why don't you look at it this way instead' won't do the trick, your reframe has to have enough impact cognitively and emotionally for the client to fully accept it. Jokes often use reframing because the punch-line makes you suddenly understand things differently, for example: two fish are living in a tank, and one says to the other, 'Do you know how to drive this thing?' I don't think I'll be giving up my day job in favour of comedy but I'm sure you get the idea. Within therapy, you can reframe past events that the client classifies as failures as ' practice runs' for example.

Post-Hypnotic suggestions: a post-hypnotic suggestion is something you ask a hypnotised person to do, which they will only act on after being brought back to normal consciousness. These suggestions often concern behaviour (emotional or physical) which is linked to a specific occurrence or situation called a trigger.

For example, a stage hypnotist might suggest that one of their volunteers will cluck like a chicken every time they hear anyone count to three. (I appreciate I'm using stereotypes here, but just go with it!) The volunteer will then be brought out of trance and sent to sit down, thinking their turn is over. As many excuses as possible will be used for the hypnotist to count from one to three during the rest of the act, and each time the original volunteer will stand up in the audience and cluck like a chicken.

They're not in hypnosis but they are responding to a post-hypnotic suggestion, by producing a behaviour (clucking like a chicken) in response to a trigger (the hypnotist counting to three). Being 'made' to act in a ridiculous way, maybe after the session is over, might be one of the things your clients worry about when they first come to see you, and if so you will need to address it in your pre-talk.

A large proportion of the suggestions we give for therapy could be thought of as post-hypnotic suggestions, since they are designed to help your clients to continue to be non-smokers, or healthier eaters, or less anxious after they leave the therapy room. For example: "Every time you see someone smoking, or notice the smell of smoke from other people's cigarettes, your own determination to remain a non-smoker becomes ten times stronger."

We can also use post-hypnotic suggestion to enhance or replace future inductions. For example

"Whenever we work together, I will begin by asking you to take three deep breaths. As you take the first deep breath you will notice yourself starting to relax. At the second you will notice that relaxation getting deeper. As you take the third deep breath you will find yourself moving immediately into a deeper and deeper level of trance every time."

Try this out: Practise the techniques

Write some more suggestions for Annie, the quit smoking client mentioned earlier in this chapter, using one or more of these techniques.

Stage hypnotists often use memory-based suggestions as part of the act (for example, suggesting that someone forgets the number three then asking them to count the number of fingers on one hand) but the effects of these suggestions are always removed at the end of the show.

In therapy, suggestions around memory must be used carefully. Clients who present asking to literally 'forget' an ex-partner for example should be encouraged to deal with the feelings the ex brings about instead. However, it can be useful to suggest that clients forget to carry out an habitual action such as smoking or overeating; the confusional language example earlier in the chapter does this. Essentially you should ensure that any suggestions you give around memory are safe and ethical.

Ethics are a major consideration at all times, of course, but need special consideration when you are constructing post-hypnotic suggestions. For example, it's not ethical for a therapist to suggest

- that the client will be unable to go into trance for anyone else in the future
- anything that undermines their dignity, self-esteem or confidence
- anything that could be emotionally or physically harmful to clients or others
- that clients will do anything illegal

Hopefully it never crossed your mind to do anything like this, but it's worthwhile making the point.

Why can't I just use a script?

Whether therapeutic scripts are an essential tool, an occasional prop, or absolutely to be avoided is a topic which is often hotly debated in social media, and other places where hypnotherapists gather to discuss their art.

The 'for' views are pretty obvious. If someone at the top of the profession is willing to tell you what they say to their clients, for example, why wouldn't you start there? Using scripts means you never go 'blank' in a session and wonder what to say next, you can take the time to craft your hypnotic language perfectly without the pressure of the client being there as you do it, and if you are newly qualified or working with an issue or technique for the first time it can give you confidence.

The arguments against scripts are that not all come from experts, some are badly designed and written. They stifle a therapist's creativity by relying on generalisations and, worst of all, they are a safety blanket for inadequate or badly trained therapists. You can, of course, get around many of these objections by writing completely original scripts for each client session, but not only does that take up a lot of your unpaid time, it will still not reflect any of the information the client gives you in the session if it's been prepared beforehand.

As with most things, the different views all have something going for them and, for me, the truth is somewhere in the middle. Even seasoned pilots use a flight checklist; no one accuses them of being poorly trained and no one would suggest that a pilot with no training or experience should be left to fly a passenger plane with only a checklist for guidance. There's no reason scripts can't be used in the same way, as a guideline rather than a straightjacket, and we're going to look at how to do this in the next chapter.

Chapter summary

"Your mind is working on your future based on a suggestion. The question is, 'on whose suggestion is it working: yours or others'?"
Assegid Habtewold
(www.goodreads.com/quotes/tag/suggestion)

Having spent so much time in creating a good rapport with your clients and getting into their world, you need to help them find ways to make changes that are consistent with that world and work within its realities. That means using the client's solutions, not your own.

It seems fair enough to start with the idea that what all nail-biters have in common is the behaviour of biting their nails, but it's less convincing to argue that they all have the same feelings and beliefs about their habit, or that it has the same meaning for them, or the same relationship with other areas of their lives. Generic scripts, however well written, rarely reflect your client's world closely enough to be used without some modification, hence the need for an understanding of what effective suggestions are, and how they work.

Even generic scripts can work as a framework around which you build your client's personalised therapy. If you like, the script is like a Christmas tree: it gives you a basic structure, size and shape, but the finished look is almost entirely down to the decorations you hang on it.

This means it is possible to use the same basic framework for more than one client, but you need to make it fresh and personal by changing the details on each occasion. So we're going to look now at exactly how you can do that.

References and footnotes

1. Author name/date not stated, suggestion, www.dictionary.com/browse/suggestion?s=t

2 .Leslie, Mitch. (2000). 'Research supports the notion that hypnosis can transform perception' in *The Stanford Report*, September 6, 2000, Stanford University: California. news.stanford.edu/news/2000/september6/hypnosis-96.html

3. Cited in Orszulok, Alice, (June 20, 2012) 'The power of suggestion'. *Science Illustrated*. http://scienceillustrated.com.au/blog/science/the-power-of-suggestion/

4. Wilson, Krissy, (2011) 'New Voices: The Power of Suggestion', in *The Psychologist*, The British Psychological Society, October 2011, 24: 782-783. Warners Midlands PLC: UK.

Chapter Four

Working with words

The point of therapy is to help your client make positive changes. Here we look at techniques for doing this which use your client's ways of understanding the world.

Many therapists begin by using therapeutic scripts from books and websites. It's a good way to tap into hypnotic language and to get ideas from more experienced therapists. Unfortunately, as we've said, one of the big problems is that they do not reflect your client's world except in very general terms. Cast your mind back to our fictitious client Annie who wanted to quit smoking because she was planning a family. Few, if any, 'quit smoking' scripts include that as a motivator, because (being generic) they are forced to concentrate on what smoking clients have in common, rather than on what makes them unique.

It's all very well to say 'adapt them', but many look complete, or have an internal flow and logic, so that it's not always easy to see how this can be done. What we're going to look at in this chapter is a way to approach that adaptation process. What information do you need to include?

We're going to use a fictitious client, who we'll call Maisie, as an example of how to adapt a script. Maisie has developed driving anxiety following a motorway accident. Her full intake information is at Appendix Two, but in this chapter I'll just be picking out relevant words and phrases to help me adapt a script.

Let's look at this in terms of our acronym, T.H.E.R.A.P.Y. The finished script should be aimed at moving Maisie from her 'here and now', where the problem exists, to her 're-imagined future', where she has reached her goal. Initially, the most effective way to do this is by focusing on the areas that Maisie herself has identified as needing to change, then support the process with 'add-ons' (homework), and a plan for future sessions which reinforces the work we've done, or takes things forward.

We then have to decide what information from the intake form needs to be included in the script, and for this we can start by looking at Brown's five areas of concern - behaviour, feelings, beliefs, meanings and relationships.

In the following table, I've gone through the information we have about Maisie, picking out specifically what she has now, and what she wants in the future. The route from one place to another, of course, is via the things she'd like to change. For these purposes, I've generally considered 'thinking' as a behaviour, although the content of thoughts can highlight beliefs as well.

The key information (Maisie example)

Behaviour
Here and now
Avoids driving and days out.
Negative thinking, expecting the worst.
Re-imagined future via desired changes.
Driving safely and calmly.
Focusing on the road/route.

Feelings
Here and now
Anxiety - nausea, tight muscles, clenched hands, heartbeat fast.
Anticipating the sensations of another collision.
Re-imagined future via desired changes.
Able to see other cars without anxiety, relaxed, calm, safe, (singing?).
Reconnecting with the enjoyment of driving.

Beliefs
Here and now
I used to enjoy driving.
Every other car on the road is likely to hit mine.
Re-imagined future via desired changes.
I'm a safe driver.
I can be safe on the roads.

Meanings
Here and now
Anxiety 'ruins' days out.
Missing out on regular trips.
Re-imagined future via desired changes.
I can go out on enjoyable trips and excursions, for example

to the coast with granddaughter or husband.

Relationships
Here and now
Husband 'frustrated' at not being able to take day trips.
Changed jobs, lower pay.
Re-imagined future via desired changes.
Happier husband (perhaps? more information needed).
Possible return to old job.

Getting more information (Maisie example)

However thorough you try to be, you may not get all the relevant information when you first interview your client. If you have completed your intake form within a session, this could be due to time restraints; if your client has completed it and sent it to you, it could be that they are simply not aware of the level of detail you need. The benefit of this exercise is that, not only does it identify information to include in your script, it will also help you highlight areas that need following up.
For example:
- Is Maisie aware of any advantages of not being able to drive herself around?
- How does she feel when she successfully avoids driving?
- How does she feel about the possibility of going back to her old job?
- What impact has her lower wage had on herself and her family?
- How does not being able to go to the Lake District affect her, practically and emotionally?
- What exactly does she mean by days out being 'ruined'?
- How does her husband let her know he feels 'frustrated'? How does she feel about this?

- Does it affect their relationship in other areas?
- How will things change when they can take trips again?

The answers to these questions will help you plan content for subsequent sessions. In the meantime, you can still refer to these ideas by restating the situation in Maisie's own words. After all, she knows what she means by 'ruined' and 'frustrated' even if you would like more detail.

Try this out:

Look through Maisie's intake form in the Appendices. What else would you have picked out to include in the table, or to ask her about in the next session?

Try this out:

Look at your notes from a client you have worked with and perform a similar analysis of the information you obtained in your first session. Would this have changed what questions you asked or what you did next?

Adapting a generic script: the basic building blocks

As we've said before, there are two main issues with using generic scripts. One is that they can't possibly reflect your client's world in any detail, and the other is that deciding how to make them do so can be confusing because they appear complete as they are.

Here we are going to go through a script in detail and I will show you how to customise it for a particular client. You can then apply the techniques to other scripts for your clients.

You can best use this script by inserting personal details where the script is talking about similar ideas, so go through it and look for places where Brown's five areas of interest are involved.

As you do this, make a note of where you might fit any other personal information that the client gave you about their situation or interests. In the example script these suggestions are in the right hand tinted box.

Here the first script is the generic version and the second script is a version customised for the client 'Maisie'. Read through both to see how I have added personal details in the second script.

1. Generic script

Now, as you relax you can begin to allow your mind to drift into a state of serenity and contentment, noticing as you do so how every muscle in your body can become loose and comfortable, how the thoughts drifting effortlessly through your mind can become gentle and calm.

Feelings: serenity, contentment
Behaviour : relaxation

And as you experience these wonderful feelings you can begin to see that the anxiety you've been experiencing was something your mind created to try to keep you safe. Anxiety has a useful purpose in the right time and place.

Meaning: anxiety has a positive purpose

It's a state of readiness, a little like keeping your car held on the clutch at a junction instead of using the brake, ready to set off at a moment's notice without the bother of finding the right gear or the biting point. When we are in a situation that might be difficult or dangerous, our unconscious mind keeps us on alert in the same sort of way, ready to take whatever action is necessary to defend ourselves or to remain safe. Unfortunately, sometimes that state of readiness is something that hangs around longer than we really need it, or perhaps our unconscious mind can't clearly see whether we need to be ready or not, so that it errs on the side of caution. And when this happens, the anxiety stops being useful and starts to be difficult to live with, just as you've found. And that is just the time to let the anxiety go.

So, imagine that you are in a beautiful garden where there is a table and chair. Sit down on the chair. On the table is a candle, a metal box, a box of matches, a small pad of paper and a pencil.

We can swap the garden for the Lake District: maybe give the option of drawing instead of writing

On each page of the paper, write a thought or worry or difficulty that your anxiety has created for you in the past, a situation that has triggered

your anxiety, or a physical sensation that you experience as part of your anxiety.
Write as many as you like, there are plenty of pages in the pad, and let me know by nodding your head when you've done that.
[*pause*] Good.

Now take each of those pages in turn and tear them out of the pad. Rip them out, no need to be careful. Tear them into pieces and drop them into the box. Light a match and drop that into the box too.

Watch as the pieces of paper begin to burn, brown lines smouldering along the edges first, then bursting into flame, bright and warm. Watch the beautiful colours of the flames as they flare briefly then die down, leaving nothing but ashes in the bottom of the box. Toss the ashes into the air and find that a gentle breeze takes them far away, drifting away from you, leaving you once more calm and serene.

She likes autumn, link flames to these colours

Perhaps you recall a time in the past, before anxiety was such a problem for you, when this state of peace and well-being was something you experienced often, perhaps you are feeling now that in those times you took it for granted, or perhaps failed to notice how very simple it is for your mind to create these wonderful feelings. But your unconscious mind is amazing and it remembers every good thought, every possible way for you to feel relaxed and calm, and it can allow you to feel those things again whenever and wherever you wish.

Feelings: peace, well-being. A generalisation which could be made more specific by linking it to past positive experiences of driving

Focus for a while on that feeling of peace and calm, becoming aware of where in your body you feel it. Maybe it's the slow steadiness of your breathing, or the steady beat of your heart. Whatever it is that you notice, allow that feeling to get stronger and stronger, more and more powerful, feel it spread throughout your body and mind,

Feelings: peace, calm. We can insert references to how the client wants to feel

finding its way into every muscle, every thought.

Now, imagine that wonderful feeling can expand from your body and mind into the world around you, forming a protective bubble or shield.
From now on that shield will remain around you, at all times, wherever you go, whoever you are with and whatever you are doing. It keeps those feelings of calm and serenity close in your thoughts and feelings, and it protects you, even in situations where your anxiety used to be a problem.

From now on you refuse to allow anxiety to control your life, you remain calm and serene at all times.

Feelings: calm, serenity, protection

And you can allow all these suggestions to sink deeply into your unconscious mind, where they can remain, changing your anxiety and your life in ways which are beneficial and helpful to you.

Beliefs: anxiety doesn't control me, positive change can happen

Adapting a generic script: weaving in personal information

Now we go through the script a second time and insert Maisie's information at the relevant points, so the finished script looks something like this: the changes are inset in italics so you can identify them easily.

2. Adapted script

Now, as you relax you can begin to allow your mind to drift into a state of serenity and contentment, noticing as you do so how every muscle in your body can become loose and comfortable, how the thoughts drifting effortlessly through your mind can become gentle and calm.

As you relax you can allow your mind to float off to an autumn day when you were painting in the Lake District in your favourite cove. Your paints and equipment are all ready. You can see the trees, and the lake, with the countryside beyond. Allow yourself to enjoy this feeling of peace and calm, notice how you can experience that familiar feeling of being lost in an experience without any particular need to think of anything at all.

Relating her feelings and behaviour when painting to her experience of hypnosis makes it feel comfortable and taps into her existing ability to 'switch off'

And as you experience these wonderful feelings you can begin to see that the anxiety you've been experiencing was something your mind created to try to keep you safe. Anxiety has a useful purpose in the right time and place. It's a state of readiness, a little like keeping your car held on the clutch at a junction instead of using the brake, ready to set off at a moment's notice without the bother of finding the right gear or the biting point.

When we are in a situation that might be difficult or dangerous, our unconscious mind keeps us on alert in the same sort of way, ready to take whatever action is necessary to defend ourselves or to remain safe.

Unfortunately, sometimes that state of readiness is something that hangs around longer than we really need it,

so that we worry about other traffic on the road or avoid driving as much as we can

Personal examples, behaviour

or perhaps our unconscious mind can't clearly see whether

we need to be ready or not, so that it errs on the side of caution, *not being able to put the risks of having another accident in their proper perspective, or realising that we should not allow one day when things went wrong to overshadow 30 years of safe driving.*

Personal example, beliefs about how safe driving is

And when this happens, the anxiety stops being useful and starts to be difficult to live with, just as you've found. And that is just the time to let the anxiety go.

So, imagine that
~~you are in a beautiful garden where there is a table and chair. Sit down on the chair bench. On the table~~
close to where you are painting, there is a wooden picnic bench and table, even if they haven't been there before. Walk across and sit down on the bench. On the table are a few items left for you by someone else who has stopped to admire this beautiful place. There is

Maisie likes sitting in her garden but we've already asked her to imagine being in the Lake District to help her 'switch off' so let's develop that

a candle, a metal box, a box of matches, a small pad of paper and a pencil.

On each page of the paper, *record* a thought or worry or difficulty that your anxiety has created for you in the past, a situation that has triggered your anxiety, or a physical sensation that you experience as part of your anxiety.

Word change, the original 'write' implies only words, we want to include images.

You can do this in images, drawings, sketches, words or abstract symbols, however you want to represent those feelings and thoughts.

Change to reflect her love of art

You could record the time when the van's brakes failed, and you were stuck in the car until the Police could free you.
And use another page to record the feelings of anxiety you've been experiencing recently, perhaps your hands clenched on the wheel, or the nausea, or the tightness around your shoulders.

Suggest some personal examples, leaving a short silence between each one so the client has time to do as you are asking.

Perhaps you want to include the fears you've had about being in another accident, those thoughts about other cars being too close or hitting you,
your feelings about the trips you've been unable to take,
your husband's frustration,
the way you felt about changing your job,
any or all of the thoughts and feelings that have caused you to avoid driving.
Perhaps you want to include other thoughts, feelings or beliefs which your unconscious mind makes available to you now, from the present or the past, which have somehow been part of being unable to travel comfortably and calmly in cars; your unconscious mind knows everything that needs to be there even if your conscious mind isn't sure.
Record as many things as you like, there are plenty of pages in the pad, and let me know by nodding your head when you've done that.
[*pause*] Good.

Include as many of Brown's areas of concern as you can, as well as practical situations.

Allowing her to include things we haven't yet identified as relevant makes the symbolic clearing more powerful

Word change to be consistent

Now take each of those pages in turn and tear them out of the pad. Rip them out, no need to be careful. Tear them into pieces and drop them into the box. Light a match and drop that into the box too. Watch as the pieces of paper begin to burn, brown lines smouldering along the edges first, then bursting into flame, bright and warm. Watch the beautiful colours of the flames, *the reds, yellows and oranges that reflect the autumn leaves around you.*

Reference back to the autumn day in the visualisation

~~As~~ They flare briefly then die down, leaving nothing but ashes in the bottom of the box.
As they do this you can feel all of your anxiety floating safely and securely out of your body. Your heart beating slowly and comfortably, your hands and shoulders relaxed, thoughts calm and serene.

Personalise the experience, desired change in feelings and behaviour

Toss the ashes into the air and find that a gentle breeze takes them far away, drifting away from you, *watching them drift out over the autumn trees, the lake and the countryside until they disappear*

Link to ongoing visualisation

leaving you completely calm and serene.

~~Perhaps you can~~
Recall a time in the past, before anxiety was such a problem for you, when you could experience this state of peace and well-being *whilst driving or being driven by others, when you could see other cars behind you and feel safe, calm and relaxed, focused on the road and the route, enjoying the drive.*

Use specific examples of past experiences, and tie into the client's re-imagined future

At that time ~~when~~ this state of peace and well-being was something you experienced often
when travelling in a car
and perhaps you are feeling now that in those times you took it for granted, or perhaps failed to notice how very simple it is for your mind to create these wonderful feelings. But your unconscious mind is amazing and it remembers every good thought, every possible way for you to feel relaxed and calm

Personal detail

whether you are driving or a passenger in a car, whether you are on a motorway or on smaller roads,

Personal detail related to goal

and it can allow you to feel those things again whenever and wherever you wish.
Focus for a while on that feeling of peace and calm, becoming aware of where in your body you feel it.
Maybe it's the slow steadiness of your breathing, or the steady beat of your heart
or the relaxation in your hands and shoulders.

Personal detail

Whatever it is that you notice, allow that feeling to get stronger and stronger, more and more powerful, feel it spread throughout your body and mind, finding its way into every muscle, every thought.
Now, imagine that wonderful feeling can expand from your body and mind into the world around you, forming a protective bubble or shield.

From now on that shield will remain around you, at all times, wherever you go, whoever you are with and whatever you are doing.
When you are at work or at home, indoors or out, walking or in the car

Personal detail

it keeps those feelings of calm and serenity close in your thoughts and feelings, and it protects you, ~~even in situations where your anxiety used to be a problem.~~

especially when you are travelling in a car, as a driver or as a passenger. From now on, you refuse to allow anxiety to control your life, *to decide when or where or how you can travel, or what job you should do. You're done with letting anxiety decide these things, and so* you remain calm and serene at all times.

Imagine yourself a little way into the future when you have been completely successful at eliminating your anxiety about travelling in cars. You are sitting in the driver's seat of your car, ready to drive to the coast, with Tara beside you. Your shoulders are relaxed, your heartbeat is slow and steady, your thoughts are calm and positive, you notice that old feeling of enjoyment in driving, of being free to travel wherever and whenever you wish is back and you welcome it like a long-lost friend.

The original script didn't include any future pacing, so we can insert it using the client's re-imagined future and goal

Pull the seat belt across and hear the click that means it is properly fitted, keeping you safe as you travel. From now on whenever you hear that seatbelt click, all these good feelings will come back to you, more and more powerfully every time you travel.

Auditory anchor - this will also be relevant when Maisie is a passenger

Imagine putting your hands loosely on the wheel, gripping it firmly enough to be able to steer, but lightly enough to release it and change gear easily, your hand muscles relaxed and comfortable and those good sensations travelling up to your shoulders.

You start the engine and hear that relaxing hum. As you set off, your mind is focused on the process of driving and on the route to the coast, you notice the warmth of the sun coming through the windows and you feel happy and contented.

And if the echo or the shadow of those old anxious thoughts and feelings tries to intrude into your life again, you can dispel it in a moment by using the calm breathing you've learned here today.

Just allow yourself to practise that here and now, and notice how much

Practise coping strategies

more deeply you can drift into that calm relaxed feeling. Let me know with a nod when you've done that. [pause] *That's good.*

You drive easily and safely, aware of your position on the road, checking your mirrors and seeing other cars, remaining calm and focused, perhaps even singing along to the radio with Tara.
You know and believe that you are a safe driver, you are safe in the car and so is Tara. Imagine yourself arriving at the coast, having a wonderful day together.
And when you've done that, give me a nod.[Pause]
Well done.

From now on, you feel safe and comfortable on every trip you take in a car, just as you used to, whether you are a driver or a passenger. You can travel on busy roads or quiet ones, motorways or side streets with equal ease.

If time allows you could omit this general paragraph and ask Maisie to imagine the journey home from the coast as well, or other journeys e.g. to the Lake District.

Whenever you hear the click of a seatbelt being fastened your unconscious mind will reinforce all the suggestions you've been given here today, so that you find yourself being able to enjoy driving again more and more easily, travelling freely as a driver or passenger.

Reinforce anchor

And now you can allow all these suggestions to sink deeply into your unconscious mind, where they can remain, changing your ~~anxiety and your life in ways which are beneficial and helpful to you.~~

behaviour, thoughts and feelings around travelling in cars, allowing you to go whenever and wherever you wish with the old feelings of security and enjoyment, to be a driver or passenger in a car with equal ease.

Personal examples

[give a moment of silence]

You have all the confidence and support you need to practice the breathing exercises you've learned here today, to drive your car around the block at least once this week, and to drive yourself to your next appointment with me. In fact the

Reinforce ability to do homework

harder you thought it would be to do these things, the easier you find it to do.

End on a positive, upbeat note

You can take a moment - right now [pause] *- to allow these changes to come into your life effortlessly and easily, to take root and grow in ways that can only make your life better, easier and happier.*

Adapting a generic script: what else could be changed?

Representational systems

In Chapter One we talked about identifying your client's preferred representational systems, in other words working out whether they preferred to think in words, images, sounds or feelings. We haven't paid very much attention to this element of Maisie's information so far.

We can make an assumption that she's fairly visual; she enjoys painting and the visual aspects of her garden. If Maisie was an actual client rather than a fictitious one, our observations of her NVC and language patterns would hopefully support this. There are places within the script where we can introduce changes to reflect this too, for example using the word 'see' instead of 'imagine', or adding more specific details of the views across her cove, and the painting she is doing as she imagines herself there.

On the other hand, she seems to be processing her anxiety kinaesthetically; she talks about swirling in her stomach, muscle tension in her hands and shoulders, and 'already feeling another impact'. To counteract this, given that it's impossible to be tense and relaxed at the same time, we can describe and anchor the kinaesthetic aspects of relaxation. This particular script pretty much did this for us, but we may still be able to tweak it a bit more by swapping a few general descriptors like 'relaxed' for some of Maisie's own words like 'happy'.

Direct and indirect suggestions

The original script is fairly direct, shown by phrases like 'begin to allow your mind to drift into a state of serenity and contentment' and 'on each page of the paper, write a thought or worry'. Since Maisie has a clear idea of what needs to change and how she wants to feel, this is probably fine for her.

If you feel your client would respond better to a more indirect approach, you can swap some of the phrases around to accommodate this.

Reframing

The generic script describes anxiety as being a readiness to respond quickly to a changing situation, like holding your car on the clutch at a junction. Many clients see their anxiety as negative or intrusive and this reframes it into something useful and protective. Maisie may be anxious driving at the moment, but she has previously enjoyed it, and seen herself as a safe, confident driver. This description is likely to be familiar and feels appropriate for her.

If her anxiety was triggered by something else, you could have swapped the comparison in the same way we swapped the garden for the Lake District. For an office worker, perhaps an overzealous security guard who starts usefully by checking passes and admitting authorised personnel only, but ends by refusing anyone admittance to the building whether they have a pass or not. The intention is protective, the building is undoubtedly safe, but the overall result is inconvenient to say the least. The alternative could come from another script, or your own imagination.

Words and phrases

We've said a lot so far about adapting the script to your client, but it's also worthwhile bearing in mind some of your own preferences as well. By this, I don't mean that you should use direct suggestion because you find it easier than indirect, or visual language because you are visual. Those elements should definitely reflect your client's world, not yours.

However, you do have to deliver the script in a way that sounds natural and sincere. Sometimes generic scripts include content that you're not comfortable with, or which doesn't sound like your usual way of speaking. When this happens your delivery will sound stilted and unconvincing.

The first relaxation induction I was given in my training included the line 'the muscles relaxing like a handful of loose elastic bands'. I really disliked that phrase and it had to go! At other times it may be a single word: 'your eyes remain shut with no effort at all' seems simple enough, but personally I think 'your eyes remain closed . . . ' has a better rhythm.

Stick to the guidelines about constructing suggestions given in the last chapter, and you can generally omit words or phrases that don't feel right, and replace them with something that's 'more you'.

Choosing the right script to adapt

We've looked here at adapting a single script to a client, but there is nothing to stop you taking elements from a number of scripts and combining them. Our generic anxiety script, for example, didn't include any future pacing so we added original material. But that could just as easily have been

Try this out:

Adapt the generic script in this chapter for one of your own clients who wants help with anxiety. If you're not working with clients at present, you can do this for someone you know who suffers from anxiety, or even for a fictional client such as a character from a soap opera.

Try this out:

Adapt a generic script you've used before using the methods shown. Again, you can do this for a real or fictional client or a friend.

imported from another script which did have this element.

You can also include ideas from scripts which, on the face of it, are not concerned with your client's presenting problem, if there are parallels. A script about social anxiety, for example, might include material which is relevant to a client with a public-speaking phobia, worries about an interview, or anxiety around an oral exam.

Finally, remember that your session content needs to be tailored to your client, and not your script. Even when personalised, the same script will not suit every client you work with simply because their presenting issues are similar, or because it has worked for you in the past. Each client is, above all, an individual and you'll need a variety of resources ready to adapt. Remain flexible, open-minded and creative, and above all be prepared to abandon your own plans and work with whatever the client brings you.

Creating original session content

When you are adapting other people's scripts, you are immersing yourself in hypnotic language and the construction of suggestions. You are applying the principles of hypnotic language and writing your own original material, even if it's only a few words, phrases or sentences woven into someone else's framework. As this process becomes more familiar, and you become more confident, you can create session content which is entirely your own work, the difference is only one of scale.

I'd suggest starting very much as you do when adapting a script. Set out a list like the one we created for Maisie at the beginning of this chapter, picking out behaviours, feelings, beliefs, relationships and meanings in terms of where your client is now, what needs to change, and where they want to be.

Brainstorm a few personal details that could be included (like Maisie's love of autumn days in the Lake District, or her tendency to process visually and kinaesthetically) and decide if you need to prioritise a particular sensory modality or direct/indirect suggestions.

In Chapter Three I included some ideas about how to write effective suggestions and, of course, these still apply when you are creating a whole-session script. However, writing your own content requires you to create a sense of cohesion which is probably already there when you are using someone else's script as a framework.

An outline, plan or 'storyboard' can be useful to help you structure your script. One of my favourite methods is to write down each of my disjointed ideas on a Post-it note, then stick them up on a wall. They can be moved around indefinitely until the overall order and structure makes sense.

Once you have a plan, you can begin to 'flesh it out' with more detailed ideas and suggestions.

Remember that the unconscious mind works through memory, emotion, and imagination. Suggestions which link these elements to the desired change will be the most powerful, for example

- tap into memories of times when the client felt, thought or behaved in a way which is the same as, or close to, their solution
- associate strong, positive emotions (using the client's words as far as possible) with the change
- ask the client to imagine their perfect future, so they know how it feels to experience it

The unconscious mind is also responsible for automatic body functions and actions which are repeated so often that they become habitual. You can utilise this by suggesting that the new responses feel comfortable and familiar, that they happen automatically or effortlessly, or that the client does not need to consciously notice them happening.

Finally, it's easiest for the unconscious mind to accept suggestions which are consistent with what we already believe; reframe information and attitudes so as to make change seem inevitable before actually suggesting the change.

Why would you write original content?

It sounds like you

We've mentioned already that some generic scripts will contain words, phrases or ideas that just don't seem comfortable to you. If you have written your own, you will be totally at ease with what it says, and it will be consistent with the way you speak throughout your session.

Job satisfaction

Hypnotherapy is a wonderful profession which pretty much comes with job satisfaction built in. Even so, generating your own session content gives your imagination and creativity a chance to shine, and it's so much more rewarding to know that your own, unique approach is helping your clients change their lives for the better.

Increasing your client base

If you create your own session content, you will never have to ask yourself the occasionally scary question, 'Have I got a script for that?' No matter how unique or unusual the client's situation, you can work with it.

Improving your creativity

Writing your own scripts can be a wonderful way to build your confidence to start adapting session content 'off the cuff' instead of preparing it in advance. Or perhaps even ditching the use of scripts within your sessions altogether. That is often a scary prospect when you are newly qualified, but once you can do it you can truly say that you are working with whatever the client gives you.

Career development

As you gain in experience, you can start to share your scripts with less-experienced therapists and help them on their way, building your reputation as an expert in your field.

Making audios

And finally, a very practical point. Many hypnotherapists

like to use audios, either MP3s or something more 'old-fashioned' like a CD; some give them to clients to support the work they do in sessions and others sell them as a second income stream and business-building tool.

Copyright[1] may be something you don't think about much when you use a hypnotherapy script from a book or website but, like all written material, scripts are copyright to their author. They come, of course, with implicit permission to use or adapt them in your therapy sessions with clients, otherwise the large number of script books on sale would be pretty much useless. However, this consent does not automatically extend to other uses.

If you record a client session as it happens and give the recording free of charge to your client for their own use, that's OK. However, it is a copyright infringement to distribute pre-recorded audios which are your reading of someone else's script, unless the script came with a clearly stated 'royalty free' agreement which gives permission for this use. This doesn't apply to the vast majority of published scripts, and the rule applies whether you charge for the audios or give them away free.

It's true that 'How would anyone know?' might cross your mind, but as ethical practitioners the probability of getting caught should not be the criterion by which we make our decisions! In any case there is another consideration. Those who listen to relaxation or hypnotic audios often buy more than one. As you are working hard to make your individual sessions as unique as possible, do you really want your audio to be the same as everyone else's? Assuming the answer is no, the best option from all points of view is to record your own material.

Try this out:

Write an original script for Maisie's driving anxiety session.

Chapter Summary

"Each person is a unique individual. Hence, psychotherapy should be formulated to meet the uniqueness of the individual's needs, rather than tailoring the person to fit the Procrustean bed[2] of a hypothetical theory of human behavior."
Milton H. Erickson
(www.ericksonfoundation.org/biography/)

Generic scripts, by their very nature, focus on what clients who present with a particular problem have in common, rather than on what makes them individuals. They use generalisations and assumptions because the authors cannot possibly know what is important to any one specific client. Having said that, if you don't feel confident enough to design session content completely from scratch, a well-written script can give you a good start, and you can adapt it for individual clients by inserting details that are meaningful to them.

Whatever script you start with, you can change, omit or add pretty much anything you like, combining elements from more than one script and inserting your own words.

There are no limitations because your clients have no limitations.

References and notes

1. Information based on a personal email to the author, from copyrightcircle.co.uk, May 2014, the rules may be different outside the UK.

2 Procrustean bed: forcing something to conform to an arbitrary and probably unsuitable or unrealistic standard

Chapter Five

Words, stories and metaphors

We all love stories and they provide a powerful way to help clients. Here I look at how to use stories and metaphors to make powerful interventions with your clients.

We have been talking about suggestions: how to construct them and how to use them in your hypnotherapy sessions. In this part of the book we are going to consider a slightly different approach.

We all love stories; as children listening to, reading or watching stories is one of our favourite things to do. We like fairy stories, stories about our families and our parents when they were young; all kinds of things that help us relate to our social and physical environment.

When you work with metaphors, you are essentially telling your clients a story. Just like stories, metaphors can draw us into them, provoking strong emotional responses, and they appeal to that part of our unconscious mind which is still childlike and enjoys learning in this way.

Although we are going to concentrate here on the creation of metaphors for the hypnotic part of your session, remember that they can be used in your pre-talk as well as during hypnosis.

Therapeutic metaphors

A therapeutic metaphor is a story, image or idea that represents the client's situation in a very indirect way, and provides a symbolic solution or reframe.

Look at this story for example:

Imagine you are standing at a fork in a road. Behind you is the path you've been on for years. It looked new and exciting when you set out, but as time went on it changed and now it's dirty, overgrown, polluted, full of rubbish. In front of you now the road branches in two, and you need to choose which way to go.

In one direction the path looks familiar and comfortable, with a gentle downward slope. It's the road that continues the way you've been going and you can try it out now in your mind. Notice how the trees are stunted and unhealthy, how the air is foggy and difficult to breathe, how you have to step around sticky, tarry patches on the road. I want you to travel down that road for a year or so in your mind and see where you will be if you continue the way you've been going. Is that the future you want to choose for yourself?

Now come back to the here and now, to the moment of choice, and look at the other path. It slopes upwards and there are rough patches and barriers from time to time, but you feel it's still worth exploring.

As you step onto it you realise that the path is much easier to travel than you thought it would be. The gentle slope takes you up and away from the bad air and poison of the path you rejected, and you feel clean, cool air entering your lungs, revitalising you, making you feel full of energy, fresh and healthy. You begin to walk more confidently and most of the barriers and rough patches simply fade away as you approach. The few that remain are easy to get around, or through, or over. Travel in your mind down that path for a year and see how it feels . . . is that a better path to choose?

Now come back to the here and now again, and make that choice . . .

I hope you realised two things as you read that through. One is that it's about the decision to quit smoking, even though cigarettes are never directly mentioned, and the other is that it could be made more powerful with the insertion of some personal details, especially at the 'one year ahead' points on the two paths.

The advantage of this approach over a suggestion like 'you completely reject the disgusting smell, taste and health risks of cigarettes . . .' is that it's empowering the client by letting them make their own choices. And if they do choose the downward path, they are telling you that they're not yet ready to quit. Perhaps there are secondary gains to continuing, or the benefits of quitting are just not strong enough; you can use your questioning and listening skills to explore this with them in or out of trance.

It's perfectly possible, and often advisable, to mix suggestions and metaphors in the same therapy session. Some metaphors, like the 'fork in the road' above, use ideas that are familiar to everyone and can be adapted to just about any client or issue, but personal metaphors often have more meaning. If the client has an interest in horses

> ***Try this out:***
>
> **Write a fork in the road metaphor, similar to the one on the previous page, about weight loss. Make a note of the places you could insert personal information before using it with a client.**

for example, a metaphor which uses riding, horses or even unicorns for those who like fantasy, will resonate with them more than one which is about sewing.

Metaphors can be 'content free', so, for example, sending away a number of parcels in a hot air balloon will allow the client to release whatever is necessary for healing without the therapist needing to specify what that is. This is particularly useful for clients who are struggling to face their issues directly, or those who seem to have an overwhelming number of therapeutic goals, especially if you are not quite sure where to begin.

Metaphors capture the client's interest, imagination and emotions; all unconscious activities. They can be difficult to analyse consciously. Combined, these attributes act to encourage the client to use unconscious processing to resolve their issues.

Getting ideas for metaphors

You can create your own unique metaphors, or start with other people's, just as you do with suggestion-based scripts. However, as you are seeking to engage the client's unconscious mind emotionally and imaginatively, you need to look for ways to make them personal and relevant.

Use fairy stories, dreams, everyday experiences, poems, news items, TV programmes or films, articles you have read. Or simply make them up from ideas that come into your mind.

Here are some useful themes to get you started:
1. Journeys – walks, rides etc. Usually you would include a choice of route (as per our 'fork in the road' metaphor) and/or obstacles which the protagonist successfully overcomes. These are great for giving the client confidence that their problems can be conquered, and for sparking off inspiration within the unconscious mind about how that might be achieved.

2. Reframing – stories which encourage the client to look at their situation in a different way, and often it's good to have a twist at the end. These are suitable for clients who would benefit from seeing their situation from a new perspective.

3. Clearing and cleansing – we used this approach with Maisie in the last chapter, when we asked her to imagine burning paper on which she had recorded the negative consequences of her car accident. You can also ask your client to blow their problems into balloons (or toss them into the basket below a large hot air balloon) and let them float away, put their problems in a bag and dispose of it, write them into a diary and burn it, or onto a computer document and delete it, imagine spring cleaning your attic, etc. This approach helps the client to identify and get rid of their problems without always having to be too specific about what they are.

4. Finding solutions – libraries, buried treasure, meeting a

wise advisor etc. Essentially, you are asking the client to find a metaphor for their own unconscious mind, and use it to obtain the solution to their problem. Avoid religious imagery for an 'advisor' unless you know the client's spiritual views, since meeting an angel might be great for believers, but not so much for sceptics.

5. Feeling protected – creating a protective bubble or shield, magic cloak etc. This kind of metaphor installs symbolic resources which help the client to feel more in control in a situation they previously thought of as a problem.

6. Controls – machines, control room, dials, thermometers, switches etc. This is a bit of a hypnotic 'classic', and used to empower the client, giving them a way of being in command of their emotions or symptoms.

7. Combined metaphors – mixing any of the above, for example, taking the client on a journey on which they have to overcome obstacles, at the end of which they meet a wise advisor who helps them to find a solution to their problems and gives them a protective device of some kind to prevent it recurring.

Using the client's metaphors

Listen out for the metaphors that your client uses and look for ways to bring them into the therapy part of your session.

If they say their stress is like being on a runaway train, then a story about trains, travel or even stampeding animals might feel right. If they say it's like a heavy weight, use a tale where someone is relieved of the necessity to carry an unnecessary burden.

The client's likes, dislikes, dreams, hobbies, job, family,

mannerisms, physical appearance or style of dress might all give you inspiration. For example, if a client is a philatelist, a story about searching for a very rare stamp might provide the basis for a solution-discovery metaphor. The only restriction is your own imagination.

Adapting other people's metaphors

You may feel that metaphors are likely to need less adaptation than suggestion-based scripts, and in some ways this is true. The same basic story can mean a lot of things to a lot of people. However, the most important thing is that the client has to identify with the character or object that represents them in the story. If they don't do this, then they will not take on the resolution that is being offered.

A few tweaks here and there will make this identification easier and pay dividends in terms of maximising the effects of your sessions. Typical 'tweaks' might include:

- ensure the client and the character that represents them (the protagonist) are the same gender
- replace some of the words describing how the protagonist feels with words that the client has used to describe their own experiences
- give the protagonist some attributes that mirror those of the client, red hair perhaps, or a love of reading
- adapt some of the descriptive portions of the story to the client's sensory preferences, adding more visual detail for clients that think in images, or more about textures and feelings for those who are kinaesthetic
- ask what kind of books or TV programmes the client likes, to help you decide whether they'll appreciate something fantastical or more based in reality.

One of the great advantages of using metaphors is that you are not the only one to be able to adapt them. Clients sometimes bring their own ideas into a metaphor in a way that would be almost impossible with suggestion.

For example, I once asked a client to imagine walking down a corridor, finding a door with her name on it and going through the door into the room behind it. She imagined the corridor with no problems, but said there was no door with her name. Instead, she described a cave at the end of the corridor with her name painted over the entrance. She said that, although she found this puzzling, she 'just knew' that was where she had to be. Her imagination supplied the image because at some unconscious level it had meaning to her, and we worked with it to great effect.

Give your clients freedom to do this when delivering metaphors, and never try to force things back into the path you had chosen. Had I said, 'Forget the cave and keep looking for the door,' I would have broken rapport as well as ignoring where the client was clearly telling me they needed to go.

Writing your own metaphors

Structure

If you are working with an original idea, begin as you did with the suggestion-based scripts, by storyboarding it along with some key words or phrases.

Try this out:

Write a 'fork in the road' metaphor and adapt it using what you know about Maisie, our fictitious client.

Metaphors, just like any stories, should have a beginning, middle and end. The beginning needs to set up the client's identification with the protagonist, the middle generally involves setbacks or problems to be overcome, and the end includes a resolution.

Your basic outline should therefore be something like this:

- Identify the situation or problem the client wants to change
- Ask yourself 'What are the most important elements of this situation?' Stick to emotions and perhaps behaviours here, the literal situation is not important
- Decide from what your client has told you what the desired outcome of therapy is, again in terms of feelings or behaviour
- Create a story involving a similar emotional problem in which the solutions mirror the client's desired goal.

Style

Remember metaphors appeal to the child within. Use everyday language, so it's easy for your client to understand.

Stories from your own experience can be presented as if they happened to someone else, or as if you read them in a book or article, to avoid self disclosure issues.

Metaphors can be first person (imagine you are standing at a fork in a road and you need to decide which way to go) or third person (a man/woman was walking along a road and came to a place where it branched into two paths). If you choose the second option, remember that the client needs to identify with the character you are talking about.

There is no need to spell out the underlying message of the metaphor. In fact, leaving some mystery encourages the client to find their own meanings and conclusions. However, adding a bit of context can help the client to begin the process of identification and see the relevance.

I often introduce metaphors within sessions with something like, 'As I was listening to you telling me about yourself today, it reminded me of a story I heard/an article I read recently . . .' which of course makes them wonder why this particular story jumped into my mind.

Putting it together

In the last chapter I showed you how to adapt a suggestion-based script to an imaginary client, Maisie, so let's run through how we can develop a metaphor to use with her as well. The first step is to use our basic outline as follows:

Identify the basic situation

Maisie used to enjoy driving, but since the accident cannot drive without anxiety

Most important elements

- Anxiety
- Loss of freedom, enjoyment
- Avoidance and excuses

Desired outcome

- Enjoy freedom again
- Feel safe and protected whilst doing so
- Feel happy

Maisie has a young grand-daughter, who she often looks after. They like to listen to story tapes on some of their car journeys, so using a fairy story structure in the metaphor will reflect her past positive experiences of driving. Here's what I've come up with. Look for the parallels as you read it through.

Maisie's metaphor

You saying that you liked to listen to stories with your granddaughter reminded me of a story I once heard about a princess who lived in a castle. Near the castle was a beautiful place filled with trees, lakes and mountains, and in a cave in the forest lived a family of dragons.

Now, many princesses have their doubts about dragons, but this one thought they were wonderful. She would visit them almost every day, she painted pictures of them against the mountains and lakes of their home, cared for and played with the babies, and she often took her family and friends to visit too.

In their turn the dragons did her many favours. They would start up fires in the castle when the wood was damp, and take her for rides on their backs far up into the sky where she could see for miles. Up in the sky it was exciting and exhilarating. She felt happy, free from the rules and restrictions that are part of every princess's life, and on dragon-back she could easily visit places that would be too far away on a horse. The Princess thought that there was nothing better than dragons.

One day she went flying with her favourite dragon. They were soaring easily on the wind currents when something happened that had never happened before. A freak gust of wind caught the dragon unawares and tumbled them both across the sky.

The Princess was really frightened. She clung tight to the dragon as he spun through the air, and finally landed badly, making his wing painful and sore. It was obvious that he wasn't going to be flying her home today. Although the

Princess wasn't hurt, she was stranded and far from home, scared, and very worried about her friend.

Eventually, the watchman on the castle tower noticed that they had disappeared from view and called for help. It seemed to take forever for the soldiers to arrive from the palace, but eventually they came. They brought a horse for the Princess to ride home and a large wagon to carry the dragon back to his family.

The Queen was very upset by what had happened. She had always had her doubts about dragons. Even though the Princess had been friends with them for years, and hadn't been hurt during the fall, the Queen felt the accident proved that dragons were simply not good things to be around. She was supposed to keep the Princess away from danger, and she needed to do a better job.

The dragon's wing was soon mended and healthy. He enjoyed spending time with the Princess, and expected to go out flying with her again, but somehow the Queen always managed to put something in the way. There was a state visit, the castle needed a spring clean, or new curtains had to be chosen for the throne room. One reason after another.

At first the Princess would find the time to go and visit her friends the dragons, but when one of them offered her a ride she had to say no because of the long list of chores she had waiting at home. To be honest, it came as a bit of a relief to have a reason. Whenever she thought about flying now, the Princess thought about that scary fall. She wasn't sure she wanted to fly any more, but every time she said no, she felt guilty about upsetting her friends. She didn’t want to feel bad, so she made excuses, and she went to see the dragons less and less until she didn’t come at all.

The Queen was happy that she was protecting her daughter so well, but soon she began to worry about other things too. After all, it's not just dragons that cause problems. She began to stop the Princess from riding her horse, or going out in her carriage, or even into the garden. She had the Princess's food cut up before it was brought to the table so she didn't have to use a knife, and one day suggested locking her up in one of the castle's spare towers . . . just to keep her away from anything dangerous, of course. From the Queen's point of view, it seemed, the Princess could never be safe enough.

The Princess understood that the Queen was trying to help, but she now saw that the real answer to a fall was to get back up on the dragon. Instead of doing that, she'd accepted one restriction after another.

Each new restriction had seemed to be only a small one, but when you added them all together the Princess didn't have much fun left in her life at all. She realised that she missed the garden, her horse, and her carriage, even cutting up her own dinner. And most of all she missed the dragons. She missed cuddling the small, warm bodies of the baby dragons and the sense of freedom and happiness she got when the older ones took her for rides.

A wise woman lived in the castle, and the Princess went to see her. The wise woman could see that if the Princess simply started to ignore the Queen's new rules it would be very difficult, because the Queen expected them to be obeyed. Another way had to be found to reassure her that the Princess was OK.

So the wise woman gave the Queen and the Princess golden bracelets to wear, each decorated with a magic diamond. The diamonds had been cut from the same stone and were still attuned to one another. The wise woman told them that, as long as the Princess was safe, the diamonds would stay clear and sparkling. And if she did get into any trouble they would both go red, so the Queen would know to come and help.

So the Princess put on her new bracelet and went to visit the dragons. She felt a bit worried about how they'd react to seeing her because it had been such a long time, but they were so pleased that they took her flying right away.

Life seemed exciting again, and as they soared through the air the Princess was very happy. She felt safe and secure knowing that if she ever needed help it would come straight away.

From the castle battlements, the Queen watched her rise into the sky and then glanced down at her bracelet. The diamond was shining, flashing brilliantly white, and she felt a surge of happiness knowing that all was well. She looked back at her daughter soaring higher into the fluffy clouds and suddenly knew that this freedom was what was right for her.

She didn't have to lock the Princess in a tower to keep her safe, but could check her bracelet as often as she wanted, staying in the background and only taking action when it was really needed.

And everyone was happy, just as anyone can be if they allow themselves to shed the boundaries they don't really need, and find the freedom and excitement in life again.

Explaining Maisie's metaphor

In this story the Princess, of course, is the client. We could have called her Princess Maisie, but that's a bit obvious. Instead we have a few details which should help Maisie to identify with her; she draws and she babysits the little dragons, and the area where the dragons live sounds a lot like the Lake District. (With a real client you could add more specific descriptions of her favourite spot for painting.) If

Maisie wore a distinctive piece of jewellery, like a ring or pendant, I'd have used this instead of a bracelet, or swapped the diamond for a gem that matched. We also know from our intake form (Appendix Two) that Maisie has no concerns about heights or flying. If she did, a metaphor about falling from the sky would be inadvisable to say the least.

The Queen represents Maisie's anxiety, tasked with keeping her safe. She's well-intentioned in that role, but unable to put risks in their proper perspective without some guidance, so her attempts at protection become unnecessarily restrictive.

The wise woman is the therapist, providing a way forward that everyone is happy with. Notice that she doesn't banish the Queen or ignore her, but instead acknowledges her value and gives her a better way of knowing when she is needed. If the role of anxiety is essentially defensive, it needs to be made less reactive rather than switched off altogether. I'd combine this metaphor with an anchor for feeling safe, probably on the client's wrist to reflect the magic bracelet.

Try this out:

Write an original metaphor for one of your clients.

Chapter Summary

"The logic of the emotional mind is associative; it takes elements that symbolize a reality, or trigger a memory of it, to be the same as that reality. That is why similes, metaphors and images speak directly to the emotional mind."
Daniel Goleman, (1996) *Emotional Intelligence.* Bloomsbury, London [p.294]

Metaphors provide a wonderful way to communicate with your client's unconscious mind. It's often said that dreams are the expression of hidden or unconscious meanings. In a way a good hypnotic metaphor is like creating a dream for your client, so that the unconscious mind can process it and respond in a much more naturalistic way than simply following suggestions.

Therapeutic metaphors allow the client to identify with the story you are telling, so that they can process the embedded suggestions and reframes without needing to be consciously aware of how that is happening. Using a few personal details and remaining aware of the client's preferred representational systems helps with this identification, and ensures the metaphors become more relevant and powerful.

Chapter Six

When worlds collide

Your ideas and those of your client may differ radically. Here I look at how you can handle this and look after yourself.

Although the chapter title is a little exaggerated, it is true that, having spent a lot of time considering your client's world, you need finally to consider the impact of your own. You do not provide therapy in a vacuum, any more than your client seeks it that way, and events in your own life will make you feel tired, happy, sad, energised, worried, excited, and so on.

Ideally, of course, these things are left outside your therapy room door when you go into 'work mode'. If you have a lot going on and think you can't do this, it's best not to practise for a while, or at least not to see clients with issues that mirror your own. If you have recently suffered a bereavement, for example, it would almost certainly be a good idea to refer on clients in the same situation. But you need to recognise that even smaller events can have an impact on your ability to get fully into your client's world and provide effective therapy. It's why looking after yourself as well as your clients is so important, and in this final chapter we are going to have a look at a few ideas which will help you do just that.

Build a library of easily adaptable scripts

Having read through this book, you might well be worrying about how much time you will have to spend in customising and writing scripts. Apart from any other consideration, your hypnotherapy is a business intended to make a profit, and you are only paid for the hours that you spend with your clients.

Although this is a fair point, offering effective, personalised therapy is good for your business in the long run. Happy and successful clients are more likely to pass your name on to others, and word of mouth is the best possible advertising. Essentially it's getting other people to do your marketing for you, and it's free . . . what more could you want?

In addition, your client could listen to a generic script from a CD purchased for a few pounds on the Internet. I've always felt that, if people are investing their time and money in coming to see you, they deserve to get more.

Like any other skill, adapting scripts does take time when you are starting out, but the more familiar you are with the process, the quicker you can work. Imagine baking a cake for the first time. You have to find a recipe you like the look of, make sure you have all the ingredients or buy them, measure them carefully, then follow the instructions step by step, double-checking all the way.

Now imagine you have made an identical cake every week for a year. Chances are you will have everything you need already in the cupboard, you only occasionally need to check the instructions, and you may not even bother weighing the ingredients.

As you adapt more scripts, you'll develop this same sort of 'feel' for where you break the usual recipe you use, and which of the client's details should be used. And you can speed up this process even more by doing some of the work in advance.

Most therapists have downtime now and then, where they are not fully booked, or a client cancels at the last minute. A really good way to use this time is to begin the process of adapting some of the scripts you use regularly. You can:

- change individual words or phrases you don't like
- identify places where you could insert personal information or details, for example where the script uses generalisations or talks about behaviour, feelings, beliefs, meanings or relationships
- look for and rectify omissions, for example our generic anxiety script didn't have any future pacing
- classify your scripts as primarily direct or indirect
- identify sections where the sensory preferences could be adapted.

If you enjoy writing your own material, you can do so on a kind of 'pick and mix' basis, writing shorter paragraphs and stories which can be linked together with a client's personal information. After a while you will have a library of templates which are easy and quick to adapt when you are fully booked with clients.

Maintain a good work/life balance

If you worked for someone else you'd take holidays and days off, but self-employment can become a 24/7 activity. You can check your work/life balance by running a kind of audit, and one way to do this is to create a 'stress account' [1]. Most accounts are there to keep track of your income and expenditure to make sure you don't overspend. The stress account on the next page is there to monitor the emotional ups and downs of your day to make sure you don't over-tax yourself.

Essentially you make up a list in two columns. (There's a pro forma to use for this in Appendix Four at the end of the book.) Log the activities and events that deplete your energies on one side and those that replenish them on the other. Assign a score between 1 and 10 to each depending on the value.

The example on the next page is showing a good day, with a healthy positive balance. The odd day 'in the red' is probably to be expected – we all have them – but if you regularly find yourself in negative figures, you can identify where the biggest or most frequent pressures come from and take action.

What actions can I take?

1. Learn to accept that things don't always have to be 100% perfect. There's absolutely nothing wrong with having high standards or setting ambitious goals, of course, but sometimes having time with your kids is more important than tweaking a client leaflet for the 40th time.
2. Put personal/relaxation time in your work diary. In one of the Winnie the Pooh cartoons, Rabbit, a control freak if ever there was one, is holding a party. One of the items on his agenda is "3.02 PM: rabbits have fun". I'm not suggesting

Try this out: score yourself

Run a stress account every day for a week. Do your scores surprise you? How could you improve them?

Your stress account

What did you do	**Was it depleting? Debit score?/10**	**Or replenishing? Credit score? /10**
Boss in a bad mood at 'day job'	**-8**	
Stuck in traffic, an hour late home	**-6**	
Hypnotherapy client reported successful week		**+9**
Putting kids to bed		**+8**
Quality time with partner		**+8**
TOTAL SCORES	**-14**	**+25**
BALANCE FOR DAY		**+11**

you go quite this far, but scheduling your family commitments (even if it's just a pizza and video night) makes it more likely you will remember to arrange client appointments around them.

3. Set specific times and days in which you will see clients and stick to them. Have a reciprocal agreement with someone whose working hours are different to yours, so you send them your daytime appointments, they send you their evening ones. If someone really pushes to see you outside your usual times, quote an out of hours rate that's above your usual fee. This often encourages them to be more flexible, but if not you are being compensated for the reduction of your personal time.

4. If your client hours are not fully booked, use that time to work on your business: prepare scripts or leaflets, write and schedule blogs, and the like. You'll have fewer calls on your time when you are busy, and these tasks will not spill out into your personal time.

5. Schedule – and take – time off. Plan ahead so clients will know you are not contactable, put a holiday message on the emails and phone, and switch them off. Think about something else!

6. Do your best to separate work and home. If you work and live in the same place, have a routine of some sort that tells your brain when to switch off. It could be something as simple as wearing 'work clothes' to see clients and even to do paperwork, then changing out of them when the work is done.

7. Have a separate phone for work so you can connect with friends and family without checking work stuff as well. Switch your work phone off at pre-arranged times.

8. Don't overload yourself: prioritise and learn to say no graciously.

Try this out: one idea at a time

Take one idea from the list and try it out to improve your work/life balance. Next week, try another.

9. Accept that it's OK to do things for yourself. Switching off and controlling your stress levels makes you more effective in the long run, not less.
10. The 'Pareto Principle'[2] says that 80 per cent of your success comes from 20 per cent of your effort. Identify which of your activities benefit you most, and focus your efforts there. Let go of those activities which achieve the least.

These are all things you would tell your clients, so remember to take your own good advice!

Make the best use of your time

Many therapists start out by running their fledgling practice alongside another job. This means making the most of the time you have for your business, so you can still have time for yourself and your family.

Lists and prioritising

Lists are great, especially if you are the sort of person who likes the visual reminder of what you've achieved which is offered by ticking off items on your list. If your list is overwhelming, or you have trouble prioritising, use a time management system.

It will take time to learn and put this in place. Probably less time than you think, but some. You might be concerned that this will just put you further behind, or give you more to do. In a way you're right, but this is only a temporary effect. Once the system is in place, it takes very little effort to keep it going, and you'll find it easier to cope with all the tasks you have to do.

Firstly, divide your list of tasks into two sets: essential (what you absolutely must do) and not essential (what you'd like to do). Then go through the two sets and divide each of them into two more: urgent and not urgent. For this exercise, urgent is anything with a deadline of ten days or less.

Just to make this clear, here are a couple of examples.

- Your MOT is due. This is essential, since without it you won't be able to get to work. If it's due in the next ten days, it's essential and urgent. If it's not due for another month it's essential and not urgent.
- You want to buy a lottery ticket. You don't usually bother, but there is a huge rollover this week and you'd like a shot at it. Your chances of winning are small, so if you don't get around to doing it there won't be huge repercussions. However, by next week the rollover will have gone; if you're

Time management chart

	Essential (Must do)	**Not Essential (Would like to do)**
Urgent **(Less than ten days)**	**I**	**III**
Not Urgent **(More than ten days)**	**II**	**IV**

going to do it at all, it has to be this week. So it's not essential, but it is urgent.

• You've always wanted to trace your family tree. You have a few ideas about where to start, but that's as far as you've got. As it stands, this would probably be not essential and not urgent. However, if you have a free membership for a genealogy website which only lasts a week, you might want to reclassify this item to urgent, so as to get the most out of the opportunity.

Now you have sorted all your tasks, make a chart using the template on the previous page. You can see that your sorting allows each task to fit into one of the four boxes and you complete them in the order shown on the chart. If you don't get to everything, it's the least important tasks that get left.

Of course, sooner or later things in the 'not urgent' part of the box will approach their deadline and become urgent or pass it altogether. To prevent them getting missed, review your tasks once a week and reclassify as necessary.

By defining urgent as anything due within ten days, and reviewing weekly, nothing should fall between the gaps. Add new tasks straight into the system as they arise. This takes just a few minutes each week and should keep you on track.

Schedule downtime

You will function better if you take regular short breaks and spend some time each week doing something for you. It's essential and urgent!

Delegation

This is a useful concept at work and at home. You have limited resources of time and energy, and need to use them wisely. Although you can't delegate your clients to anyone else, there may be other tasks that can be passed on. Paying someone to look after your accounts or website, clean your home or weed the garden, even if it's just occasionally, might be worth it. Compare the benefits of having one less task to do with the financial outlay and make the best decision for you.

Streamline your tasks

It's a sad truth that tasks tend to expand to fill the time you give them. Allocate specific time limits to tasks and stick to them. Be realistic about what time it will take to do a good job, but don't procrastinate or allow yourself to endlessly 'tweak' tasks or get distracted. Chunk large or complex tasks into smaller ones, just as you would with client's goals, and take it one step at a time.

Try to 'batch process' jobs, so that rather than writing a new post for your Facebook page every day, and a new blog every week, you write a month's worth of material at one time and schedule it to be published when it's due.

Focus on one thing at a time. If you are writing a blog, do just that. Switch your emails and social media off, so you are not tempted to break off and check them.

Get the right support

Supervision

Many industries, especially the caring ones like nursing and counselling, expect their practitioners to be in supervision, which is described by the General Hypnotherapy Register as:

"Meetings with a colleague (or colleagues) to discuss, in confidence, ongoing cases and issues arising from them, and

Try this out: manage time

Set up a time management system to help streamline your business and home activities. If you don't like the one we've outlined, you can find others online.

to work through any personal matters that might affect their own position or ability as practising therapists."[3] For UK hypnotherapists, your professional body will almost certainly make this a compulsory process, at least at the beginning of your career, and career-long supervision is strongly encouraged.

My driving instructor used to say he would teach me to pass my test and I'd learn to drive after that. He was right. Hypnotherapy practitioner training is similar because, however good it is, it can't give you experience. The period following graduation can be a very steep learning curve, especially if you haven't been self-employed before. During training, you always had your tutor to turn to. Once qualified, your supervisor takes over that role, offering help and support when you need it. Supervision is often thought of as 'where you go when you don't know what to do with a client', but there should be so much more to it. Supervisors work in different ways, but there are generally three main goals to supervision:

- developing your professional skills, abilities and understanding of practice, including how you work with individual clients
- offering you emotional support if needed, and ensuring that you have appropriate self-care procedures in place
- improving the safety and effectiveness of your practice,

for example ensuring that you work ethically, and keep yourself up to date with relevant changes in the regulations or law affecting your practice

You can see that this is very important, and a good supervisor can have a huge impact on how well you work with clients. As therapists, we are bound by rules of confidentiality and can't go home and share our day with family as you might in other jobs. Supervision is a safe place to discuss the practical and emotional impact your practice has on you, to explore where things are going right and where they could be improved, and to get advice from someone more experienced.

Most professional bodies have a list of approved supervisors and will provide this on request. Don't automatically pick the nearest or the cheapest. Going back to my driving instructor analogy, they can all get you through your test, but, as you are going to be spending a lot of time in the car with them, you need someone on your wavelength.

My advice is to ask other therapists about their supervisors, contact several people from the supervisors list, and find someone who will provide you with just the right balance of challenge and support. In other words, choose a supervisor as you would like your clients to choose a therapist.

Keep on learning

Your professional body is also likely to have targets for Continuous Professional Development, or CPD.

Supervision is about reviewing skills you already have to make sure you are using them effectively, and often also helps to identify areas where more knowledge would be useful. CPD is the process of actually acquiring that knowledge; either learning new skills, or consolidating and improving existing ones. It can take the form of training courses and workshops, but also includes activities such as reading books and articles, research, and attending webinars and conferences.

CPD is a great way of keeping your practice and your thinking fresh and innovative by giving you new ideas, reminding you of what you already know, and mixing with other therapists who might take a different approach from yours. This is exactly what you need when you focus on treating each client as an individual instead of trotting out the same old routine for each one.

A good CPD portfolio has a variety of activities and subjects across the year. Hypnotherapy will probably be the main topic, and you can vary between learning more about issues you already work with or branching out into new areas. Many people like to spend some CPD hours on other topics like business-building, first aid, or techniques which might complement your hypnotherapy, such as coaching or stress management.

Most professional bodies seem to leave you reasonably free to choose what CPD you feel you need. A few have accreditation procedures and will only count hours spent on activities they have pre-approved. As with most things, the answer is to check with your own professional body before signing up.

Reflective practice

Reflective practice means looking at the work you have done, and thinking about it analytically. What went well? What could have gone better? Why might that be? It's a learning process, so you are always monitoring your own progress as well as that of your clients. Linda Finlay[4] points

out that organisations tend to define reflective practice differently, but goes on to say that in general it involves:
"*. . .examining assumptions* of everyday practice. It also tends to involve the individual practitioner in being *self-aware* and *critically evaluating* their own responses to practice situations. The point is to recapture practice experiences and mull them over critically in order to gain new understandings and so improve future practice." (Finlay's emphasis)[5]

As you can see, reflective practice is a kind of self-supervision and, in fact, it can help you decide which cases to take to your supervisor.

Essentially it means reviewing each client or session to become aware of things like:

- how you are reacting to your client and whether transference or counter-transference might be a part of your relationship (if you are not aware of these terms, see Appendix Three at the end of the book)
- how well you feel you are entering into their unique world and whether this could be improved
- how you are choosing to work with them, and whether this is primarily dictated by their needs or your own (for example, are you avoiding certain approaches because you don't want to risk an abreaction?)
- how successful therapy has been and whether this could have been improved
- whether this client has made you aware of any learning points to take forward to other clients, or helped you to identify a need for further training or support.

There is nothing to stop you putting together a pro forma on this and completing it as part of your client records every time you see a client.

Chapter summary

"Don't sacrifice yourself too much, because if you sacrifice too much there's nothing else you can give . . ."
Karl Lagerfeld (www.goodreads.com/quotes)

Have you ever listened to the safety talk on a plane? Just as you are about to set off, one of the cabin crew tells you what to do if it all goes horribly wrong. It's not the greatest start to your holiday, especially if you're a worried flyer anyway, but my point is this: if, in an emergency, the oxygen masks come down, you are advised to put on your own before your children's.

That might seem counter-intuitive but it works very well. If you are safe and conscious you can do more for your children than if you are neither. Much the same principle applies to providing effective therapy.

We've talked a lot in this book about how important it is to get into your client's world, build rapport, and work from their perspective rather than your own.

Although that's perfectly true, you will provide the best service to your clients if you recognise that you too have a unique world, and what goes on there can have an impact on how you provide therapy. If you are burnt out, exhausted or emotional you will be unable to offer the personal, focused and creative approach that your clients look to you to provide. Self-care and the right attitude are therefore essential parts of providing effective therapy.

This can include:

- using slow times to prepare a library of scripts, so you are not overwhelmed when you are busier with clients
- maintaining a good work/life balance
- following the excellent advice you give your clients

- using your time and energies wisely
- taking full advantage of the resources and support offered by supervision, reflective practice and CPD.

Even if you do all these things, it's also good to reconnect with why you wanted to be a therapist in the first place. Being a therapist and spending your working life helping others is a great way to earn a living, but you can be in danger of taking it for granted after a while.

You can use the technique below with any highlights of your therapy career, of course, reminding yourself of the excitement you felt at those times. Useful moments to tap into include getting your certification, and your first successful client or even your most challenging one.

Keeping those thoughts and feelings fresh and strong in your mind helps you remain focused, flexible and effective as you work with your clients.

Try this out: looking back

find somewhere comfortable to sit, close your eyes and allow your mind to drift back to the moment you found out you had been offered a place on your practitioner's training course. How did it feel to know you were on your way?

References and notes

1. Stress Account © Kathleen Roberts, used here with kind permission of the creator.
2. Author name/date unstated, *Pareto Principle,* https://en.wikipedia.org/wiki/Pareto_principle [accessed September 2016].
3. General Hypnotherapy Register *Code of Ethics paragraph 31a,* http://www.general-hypnotherapy-register.com/code-of-ethics/ [accessed August 2016].
4. Finlay, Linda (January 2008) *Reflecting on 'Reflective practice' a discussion paper prepared for PBPL CETL* (Open University) http://www.open.ac.uk/opencetl/sites/www.open.ac.uk.opencetl/files/files/ecms/web-content/Finlay-(2008)-Reflecting-on-reflective-practice-PBPL-paper-52.pdf [accessed September 2016].
5. Ibid page 1

Appendix One: SMART Goals

Your client will have come to you with some goal in mind, something about their world that they want to change. We said in Chapter 2 that step one of therapy is challenging this in three ways.

The first is to check that the goal is focused on what they do want, rather than what they don't, in other words to ensure it is phrased as a positive intention. For example, 'I want to be confident', rather than 'I don’t want to be anxious'.

But even this can be a bit vague. What do they mean by 'confident'? How will they know when they are there? You can clarify some of this by asking 'meaning' questions, but the more specific you can be, the easier it is to get there. This means the best goals are SMART goals. This means they should be:

- Specific – I want to weigh nine stone, rather than I want to lose weight.
- Measurable – some goals, such as weight loss, are relatively easy to measure. For others, it’s more challenging. Using SUDS (Subjective Units of Distress Scale) is generally the way to go. Essentially, this involves asking the client to rate their feelings on a scale of one to ten (or whatever scale seems appropriate). It’s often best to rate a desired characteristic rather than an unwanted one, because it helps to keep the positive elements of the goal in mind. Keep a record of the client's SUDS scores in your client notes, so you can demonstrate improvement over time.

- Achievable – in other words, realistic. This will vary from one client to another. Saying 'I want to run a marathon next month in under four hours thirty minutes' is specific and measurable, but not achievable if your client is very overweight and has only just started exercising. If they've been doing marathons for years and their personal best is currently four hours thirty-two minutes, it probably is.
- Relevant – it should be beneficial and helpful to the client. Again this is going to vary from one client to another, but you can always ask, 'What will achieving this do for you?'
- Time-bound – you should set a realistic time limit to achieve the goal. This might be a specific date, a length of time, or 'within x (number) of hypnotherapy sessions'. Doing this keeps both you and the client focused and on track, though it may have to be renegotiated if, for example, unforeseen circumstances arise or your therapy plan is amended. This is an ethical as well as practical issue, since the code of ethics of most reputable professional bodies prohibit you from unnecessarily prolonging therapy.

Appendix Two: Client Intake Details

Client's name Margaret Browne

What do you prefer to be called? Maisie

Address 23 Acacia Ave, Newtown

Phone 0123 456789

OK to leave messages? Y/~~N~~

Email maisieb@newtown.net

Preferred method of contact: phone

Age 53

Medical history/medications

/contraindications No regular medications, healthy, no contraindications.

Family situation Happily married to Bob, two grown-up children (Hattie and Phoebe), one grandchild (Tara), aged seven for whom she regularly baby-sits.

Job Part time in a local newsagents, not dream job but convenient hours and she enjoys chatting to customers.

Hobbies/interests Painting (belongs to a local club); her garden, Bob does the hard physical work, but she enjoys looking at the flowers while she has her coffee in the mornings; pottering around with the family – especially having days out with Tara when she is babysitting.

Favourite place to relax Windermere, often goes there to paint, a small cove with lovely views over the lake and trees, countryside etc beyond, likes it best in autumn because of all the colours. Loves the sense of calm and peace there, always at ease with herself, often lost in the process of painting, time just passes without her needing to think about anything else.

Unrelated phobias Spiders

Lifestyle:

diet reasonably healthy

exercise regular walks with Bob

smoker never

alcohol occasional

recreational drug use no

sleep patterns good

Significant events in the last 12 months? Car accident around six months ago, changed jobs shortly after this as her previous job involved a lot of driving to see clients.

Any history of trauma? Just the recent accident

Previous hypnotherapy or other talking therapies? None

Goals of therapy To be able to drive comfortably again

Test 1 (positive) yes

Test 2 (SMART) no - adapted following client's reimagination of the future - 'to feel calm and safe driving, and to measure this by driving my grand-daughter to the coast within 6 weeks'

Test 3 (chunking) the client can be set

homework tasks of driving short distances and

gradually build up to longer ones

History to Here and Now

I have driven for about 30 years without even a minor accident, driving was part of my previous job and I really enjoyed it. About six months ago I was involved in an accident on the motorway. It wasn't anyone's fault, there was a van whose brakes failed and the driver lost control. The van skidded across the road and into the back of my car. No one was seriously hurt, but my car buckled and I couldn't get out. I had to sit there for around an hour till the Police cut me free. I felt quite calm at the time, but once I was out I got very upset.
I now get very anxious when I'm driving, especially if there's a vehicle behind me. The closer they are, the more I worry. I thought it would pass after a while but it hasn't. Motorways are the worst. My anxiety is 10/10 if there is another car behind me, probably 9/10 if not. But I've been getting the anxiety on other roads (around 7/10) and when I'm a passenger as well (around 6/10).
My anxiety makes me feel nauseous. It's a horrible swirling feeling in the pit of my stomach, I'm aware of all my muscles tensing, especially around my shoulders, as if I'm already feeling another impact. Sometimes my hands are clenched around the wheel so tight it's an effort to let go when I have to change gear. My heart beats really fast and my thoughts race, mostly panicky things like:

'He's too close' or 'He's going to hit me' when another car is behind me.
I've coped by avoiding driving. I changed my job so I could walk to work and not have to drive when I am there. I quite enjoy the new job but didn't really want to change as I earn less now. My husband is getting frustrated as well. We often used to go off to the Lake District for the weekend and now I can't go. The anxiety of the drive ruins it for me.

Establish what needs to change

I need to stop avoiding driving, especially on motorways. I need to stop worrying that every other car on the road is likely to hit mine and accept that I can be safe driving, that this was an accident which is unlikely to happen again.
I'd really like to enjoy driving again, but if that's not possible I'd like to feel calm and safe when I drive and when I'm a passenger.

Re-imagine the future

I'm driving my granddaughter to the coast, on one of the days I'm babysitting over the summer holidays. I can hear the hum of the car engine. It's a relaxing sound. I can feel the warmth of the sun through the car window. I'm happy behind the wheel, my shoulders are relaxed, and my hands. I'm a safe driver and realise the accident was just bad luck, not likely to happen again.
Tara likes to listen to story tapes or Disney soundtracks on long journeys and I might be singing along with her, but most of my thoughts are on the road ahead and the

route. Although I'm checking in the mirrors for other cars, I feel calm and safe even when they're close.
In the long term, I might consider going back to my old job which pays better than the current one.

Add-ons and aggravations

1. I will practice my breathing exercises every day to help me feel calm. (Do this in quiet times at the shop.)
2. I'm going to drive around the block at least once this week and drive myself to my hypnotherapy appointment next week.
3. I might chicken out of actually driving if it's left to me, but I can tell Bob or one of my daughters I am planning on doing it. They'll encourage me and come with me, if I need them to. I could go early on Sunday morning when there's not much traffic.

Planning

Although the main issue is driving on motorways, the client also feels anxious on smaller roads or as a passenger.
This session - begin work on alleviating symptoms and tapping into past good driving experiences. Identify anxiety reduction strategies that are safe to use whilst driving, such as breathing techniques and anchoring.
Future sessions - increase confidence in her capability as a driver. Use parts or regression to check that the accident was not tapping into any earlier experiences, watch for secondary gains connected with not being able to drive or change of jobs.

Yomp ahead

1. Teach breathing exercise which is safe to use whilst driving.
2. Start to challenge boundaries set by anxiety.
3. Use hypnosis and adapted anxiety script.
4 Set anchor of calm and safe whilst driving.

Appendix Three: Transference and Counter-transference

Transference is a concept from psychoanalytical therapy, in which someone takes their feelings about a person or object and transfers them to someone or something similar.

We all do this every day. For example, if you meet someone who reminds you of your best friend, you may be predisposed to like them. If they remind you of your overbearing and aggressive boss, you may treat them warily or distantly. It's said that when Walt Disney was looking for the voice of Snow White, he listened to candidates sing from behind a screen, so he wasn't influenced by whether they were like the cartoon character. In some ways this is an attempt to avoid transference. However, as it's generally an unconscious process, we are often not aware of making these assumptions, let alone of where they come from.

Within the therapeutic relationship, transference is generally used about a client reacting in this way to the therapist. When clients are referred by their GPs for counselling, they may have little or no say in who they see. But as a self-employed hypnotherapist, your clients choose to work with you. Their choices can be influenced by practicalities such as price, geography, or your working hours, but they will also be influenced by the client's perceptions of you based on what they know before they pick up the phone. It may be because you remind them of someone else who helped them, or who was a friend or a trusted authority figure. And once you meet and begin to work together this can become stronger (or maybe not, depending on whether you meet their expectations).

As a caring therapist, you may be the only person in the client's life who is supportive and non-critical, or in a more practical way you may be their only social contact.

In part, because of this, transference is considered by many to be a normal part of the therapeutic relationship. It may result in a client experiencing a 'crush' or sexual attraction, mistrust, anger, over-dependence, over-compliance and many other feelings towards the therapist. Psychodynamic therapists often use transference as an aid to identifying unresolved unconscious feelings and conflicts, and consider it part of the therapy the client is undergoing. Therapists who do not follow the psychodynamic model must still be aware of the possibility that some of the stages of healing through which the client passes may involve transference.

Counter-transference is a similar process but it works in the other direction, when the therapist transfers some of their own preconceptions or issues onto the client. It's an inevitable part of being human that we might 'like' some clients more than others, or feel that we might have been friends if we had met under other circumstances.

Perhaps they remind us of someone we already know and are fond of, or perhaps they share similar interests or attitudes to ourselves. This can lead us to treating them more as a friend than a client, and perhaps even prolonging therapy in order to continue the relationship.

Equally they may remind us of someone we dislike or find overbearing, or their situation somehow echoes events and feelings we are experiencing ourselves. Then we may find ourselves dreading their appointments or avoiding discussing certain aspects of their problems.

However, in therapy we are building a professional relationship and not a friendship. Counter-transference can lead to a blurring of those boundaries and too much self-disclosure, even complicity in continuing the client's maladaptive behaviours (for example, because we share them or don't want to upset the client by challenging them).

Transference between you and your clients can sometimes be seen by looking at the repetitive elements of your relationship. So, for example, if your client takes every question as a criticism, or prefers to chat socially than to explore their issues, it's an area worth exploring.

The direct approach is often the best one, as long as your concerns are expressed constructively, and with specific examples. 'It seems to me that you sometimes feel I'm being unsupportive when I ask you to come up with your own solutions to challenging situations. There was an example a few minutes ago when I asked what you could do instead of being upset when your partner criticises you unfairly. If so, I want to make it clear that that isn't my intention, and maybe work out why it seems that way. How would you like to approach that?'

You also, of course, need to be honest with yourself about your own reactions to your client. If you find yourself colluding in their avoidance of certain areas, or dreading their appointments, you need to think about why by asking questions like:

- Is this response my usual one?
- Does this client remind me of anyone else?
- Do I have any particular feelings towards them?
- Do I feel differently about this client than about others? If so, how?
- Are my feelings affecting the way I work with this client?

It's worth taking these questions to supervision as well, and possibly considering whether a referral is the best way forward for your client. Transference and counter-transference are unconscious mechanisms and cannot be avoided, but if they are consciously recognised it's possible to reduce or remove any negative or restrictive impact they have on your relationship with your clients. You may even be able to use them constructively to improve progress.

Appendix Four: Stress Account

Log the activities and events that deplete your energies on one side and replenish them on the other.
Assign a score between 1 and 10 to each, depending on the value.
Tot them up at the end of the day to see if you are in credit – or in the red!

If you're in the red – what are you going to do about it?If you're in the black – how much more capital can you accumulate?

(You can download this from the website)

What did you do? Event or activity	Depleting? Debit score /10	Replenishing? Credit score/10
Total scores		
Balance		

Other resources

Author's websites

www.yorkshirehypnotherapytraining.co.uk
Multi-Accredited Foundation and Practitioner level training in hypnotherapy, supervision for qualified hypnotherapists

www.cpd.expert
CPD opportunities for those who are already qualified as hypnotherapists and other therapy training

hypnotherapytrainingblog.blogspot.co.uk
Hypnotherapy Training and Practitioner, a free on-line magazine for hypnotherapists in practise and in training

www.theirworlds-yourwords.co.uk
Website supporting this book, see below for further information.

www.debbiewaller.com
Hypnotherapy practice

Special opportunities for readers of this book

In the private area of the Their Worlds, Your Words website is free bonus material including:

- a client intake form designed around using T.H.E.R.A.P.Y.
- a reflective practice pro forma
- a 'control room' metaphor script with guidance notes to help you adapt it to your clients
- a stress account pro forma

To gain access to these resources, correctly answer the following questions and send them to debbie@theirworlds-yourwords.co.uk
You will be sent your log-in details, normally within 48 hours and also I'll sign you up for my free monthly newsletter giving hints, tips, news and discounts to hypnotherapists and hypnotherapy students. You can unsubscribe from this at any time, and still access the bonus material.

The questions

1. Who carried out the Stamford University study on brain activity and suggestion mentioned in Chapter Three?
2. What are the names of Maisie's two daughters? (Stated in her intake form.)
3. How did the wise woman reassure the over-protective queen?

References

Brown, J. E. (1997), 'The Question Cube: A Model For Developing Question Repertoire In Training Couple And Family Therapists' in *Journal of Marital and Family Therapy*, 23: 27–40. doi: 10.1111/j.1752-0606.1997.tb00229.x

Claridge, Jack. (18.3.2016) *Universal Body Language Features*. http://www.bodylanguageexpert.co.uk/universal-body-language-features.html [accessed May 2016]

Denton, Cheryl. (14.2.2011) 'Why do I feel so guilty?' on *Hope Among the Ashes*. http://hopeamongtheashes.blogspot.co.uk/2011/02/why-do-i-feel-so-guilty.html [accessed June 2016]

Finlay, Linda. (January 2008) *Reflecting on 'Reflective practice' a discussion paper prepared for PBPL CETL* (Open University) http://www.open.ac.uk/opencetl/sites/www.open.ac.uk.opencetl/files/files/ecms/web-content/Finlay-(2008)-Reflecting-on-reflective-practice-PBPL-paper-52.pdf [accessed September 2016]

General Hypnotherapy Register. *Code of Ethics paragraph 31a*, http://www.general-hypnotherapy-register.com/code-of-ethics/ [accessed August 2016]

Harrison, Chris. (2008:2012) *Eye Accessing cues*, http://www.planetnlp.com/nlp_eye_accessing.html [accessed May 2016]

References

Howes, Ryan PhD, ABPP. (8.12.2010) *Silence in Psychotherapy: The talking cure without talking*. https://www.psychologytoday.com/blog/in-therapy/201012/silence-in-psychotherapy [accessed May 2016]

Karr, Laura Jean. (2013) *Cultural Body language differences*. http://www.brighthubeducation.com/language-learning-tips/4599-cultural-differences-in-common-body-language/ [accessed May 2016]

Leslie, Mitch. (2000). 'Research supports the notion that hypnosis can transform perception' in *The Stamford Report,* September 6, 2000, Stanford University: California. http://news.stanford.edu/news/2000/september6/hypnosis-96.html [accessed May 20916]

Lewis, Abigail V. (2013) 'Reflective Practice: what is it and how do I do it?' in Journal of Clinical Practice in Speech-Language Pathology, 15(2), 70-74. Posted at http://ro.ecu.edu.au/ecuworks2013/846 [accessed August 2016]

Mehrabian, Albert. (2009). ""Silent Messages" – A Wealth of Information About Nonverbal Communication (Body Language)". in Personality & Emotion Tests & Software: Psychological Books & Articles of Popular Interest. Los Angeles, CA: self-published.

Miller, Philip. (2008) *Really Good Cartoon Book of NLP.* Crown House Publishing: Wales

References

Orszulok, Alice. (June 20, 2012) 'The power of suggestion'. *Science Illustrated*. http://scienceillustrated.com.au/blog/science/the-power-of-suggestion/ [accessed June 2016]

Rouw & Schulte. (2007) cited in *Synaesthesia Research*, University of Sussex, http://www.sussex.ac.uk/synaesthesia/faq [accessed May 2016]

Wertheim, Edward G. Ph.D *The Importance of Effective Communication*, Northeastern University, College of Business Administration, retrieved 10/10/08 from http://web.cba.neu.edu/~ewertheim/interper/commun.htm [accessed May 2016]

Wilson, Krissy. (2011) 'New Voices: The Power of Suggestion', in *The Psychologist*, The British Psychological Society, October 2011, 24: 782-783. Warners Midlands PLC: UK. http://thepsychologist.bps.org.uk/volume-24/edition-10/new-voices-power-suggestion [accessed May 2016]

author/date unstated, *Biography of Milton H. Erickson*, The Milton H. Erikson Foundation. https://www.erickson-foundation.org/biography/ [accessed May 2016]

References

author name/date unstated, metaphor,
http://www.dictionary.com/browse/metaphor
[accessed August 2016]

author name/date unstated, *Pareto Principle*,
https://en.wikipedia.org/wiki/Pareto_principle
[accessed September 2016]

author name/date unstated, *suggestion*,
http://www.dictionary.com/browse/suggestion
[accessed June 2016]

author/date unstated, *Yomp*,
https://en.wikipedia.org/wiki/Yomp
[accessed May 2016]

Index

Absolutes 33, 34

Add-ons and aggravations 51

Anxiety script 82
Adapted version 88

Assumptions 33

Audios 107

Avoidance 33

Brown's Question Cube 40
Areas of interest 42

Clarifying 27

Clean language 37

Communication: understanding 25

Confusional language 69

Continuous Professional Development (CPD) 138

Copyright 108

Counter-transference 154

Don’t know the answer 44

Index

Double binds 68

Embedded commands 68

Empathy 14

Establish what needs to change 50

Eye accessing cues 31

False memory syndrome 38

Feeling reflections 26

Generalisations 34

Goals 48
Chunking 48

Grove, David 38

History to here and now 49

Incomplete information 34

Intake interview: forms and what to ask 47

Leading questions 38

Listening skills 23, 28
Levels of attention 23

Index

Lists and prioritising 133

Maisie, fictitious client, 76, 147

Mehrabian, Albert 21

Memory-based suggestions 71

Metaphors 111
Adapting 117
Client's own 116
Definition 111
Maisie's 121
Structure 118
Style 119
Themes 114, 115
Writing 118, 120

Michael, Robert 61

Mirroring 26

Modalities (see Representational systems)

Non-verbal Communication (NVC) 15
Images as non-verbal communication 20
Space as non-verbal communication 19
Visual non-verbal communication 17
Vocal non-verbal communication (paralanguage) 17
Tactile non-verbal communication 17
Time as non-verbal communication 18

Pacing and leading 27

Index

Paralanguage 17

Paraphrasing 26

Personal space 19

Planning therapy 52

Post-hypnotic suggestions 69

Question formats 40
Closed questions 41
Forced-choice questions 41
Open questions 40
Ranking questions 41
Rating questions 42

Question orientation 43

Question subjects 42

Rapport 13

Reflective practice,139

Reframing 69, 102

Re-imagine the future 51

Representational systems 29, 101
Indicators 31

Index

Restating 26

Scripts:
Adapting 75, 81, 88
Fork in the road 112
Library 128
Key information, identifying 77
Choosing 103
Creating, original session content 105, 107,
Pros and cons 71

Second and subsequent sessions 53

Self care 127
Support 136

Silence, use of 18

SMART goals 48, 145

Spiegal, David 60

Stress account 131, 159

Suggestion: 59
Direct and indirect 62, 102
Developing 65
Power of 59
Suggestions and memory 71

Summarising 53

Index

Supervision 136

Sympathy 14

Synaesthesia 30

T.H.E.R.A.P.Y. 46, 76

Terms and conditions 47

Testing the goals 48

Therapy (defintion) 58

Time management 134

Transference 154

Unrealistic expectations 34

Wertheim, Edward 16, 20

Work/life balance 130

Yes sets 68

Yomp ahead 52

their world your words

Printed in Great Britain
by Amazon

46210225R00102